# SPIRITS OF THE WILD

# SPIRITS

CLARKSON POTTER/PUBLISHERS
NEW YORK

# OF THE WILD

### THE

### WORLD'S

### GREAT

### NATURE

### MYTHS

*Gary Ferguson*

**ALSO BY GARY FERGUSON**

*The Yellowstone Wolves: The First Year*
*Walking Down the Wild*
*New England Walks*
*Northwest Walks*
*Rocky Mountain Walks*

Published by Clarkson N. Potter/Publishers, 201 East 50th Street, New York, New York, 10022. Member of the Crown Publishing Group.

Random House, Inc. New York, Toronto, London, Sydney, Auckland

http://www.randomhouse.com/

*Book design by Jane Treuhaft*

Printed in the United States of America
Library of Congress Cataloging-in-Publication Data
is available upon request.

ISBN 0-517-70369-6
10  9  8  7  6  5  4  3  2  1
First Edition

FOR *my brother Jim*

# ACKNOWLEDGMENTS

MY SINCERE THANKS to the dozens of dedicated folk-lorists and mythologists, whose tireless efforts made this collection possible. Also to my agent, Jeanne Hanson. And to my editor, Eliza Scott; my designer, Jane Treuhaft; and my illustrator, Douglas Smith, who worked so hard to make the book beautiful. Finally, thanks to the staff of the Indiana University Folklore Collection—quite simply, one of the finest resources of its kind in the world.

# CONTENTS

## TALES FROM THE HEAVENS

## THE MAKINGS OF EARTH

## THE NATURE OF THINGS

# SPIRITS OF THE WILD

# INTRODUCTION

*After you have exhausted what there is in business, politics, and so on—have found that none of these finally satisfy, or permanently wear—what remains? Nature remains.*

*Walt Whitman*

POET ROBERT FROST said that most of the changes people think they see aren't really changes at all, they're just ancient truths, passing in and out of favor. Whether they rise in the skies of Africa or from the rivers of New England, the highlands of Tibet or the jungles of Brazil, be they fanciful or shocking or funny or tragic, the great nature tales of the world whisper to us about one of those old truths: that humans will always feel the need to celebrate the possibilities of creation. Wax kin with the earth. Walk the roads that lead toward home.

Sometimes I regret having grown up in a time and place where stories from other cultures about how the world came to be were seen as quaint at best, ridiculous at worst, the shadowy leavings of simple, timid minds. It took a lot of unlearning to recognize that just because we chose to prune our own narratives to the point that all we have left are explanations of how things work, hardly means that other people would have wanted to do the same. We are spun around the dance floor by our frantic need to know what's real, all the while touting our fever as the cream of curiosity. But what if on occasion we could leave "how" and "why" out in the car with the doors locked, put a completely different tune on the jukebox, waltz for a time with the lively, footloose pleasures of invention?

Our journey begins not when the world was young— when trees married one another and animals could speak and hare climbed up to heaven on a spiderweb to steal the sun. Rather, the first steps to myth always come in the here and now, in the restlessness of our longing to grow the world. To see what lies beyond the sure thing, the right and the wrong, the black and the white; to recast life in frames big enough to hold some greater measure of wonder, a slice or two of mystery, a sip of soul.

# SPIRITS

## *of the*

# TREES

## *and*

# FLOWERS

# TULIPS

(CELTIC, NORTHERN EUROPE)
*Flowers have long been intimately connected to spirits and deities. In some myths they're treated as precious gifts to humans, each and every bloom rising from the tears or blood of the gods and goddesses. In this tale England's mystical pixies express their own pleasure and pain through the plying of tulips.*

A LONG TIME AGO, when the north of England was yet wrapped in grand sweeps of forest, when nearby meadows wore nothing but the scent of wildflowers, it was common to stumble across the antics of the little people, sometimes known as pixies. Now, pixies had no cradles for their infant children, so at night they would often place them to rest in the cups of woodland flowers. Late one evening, while out walking along the edge of the forest, a kindly old woman happened to look down into a tulip and see one of these tiny babes, fast asleep in the chalice of the bloom. This discovery so delighted her that the next morning she set about planting hundreds of tulips in her garden, until there were more than enough cradles for all the fairy folk. Many a night she would steal into her garden by the light of the moon, just to sit and watch as the breeze rocked the little ones to sleep.

In time the fairies rewarded the woman's kindness—first by making her tulips grow very large, and then by painting their petals in brilliant colors. Finally, they blessed the tulip with a glorious perfume, a scent that some say was every bit as sweet as that of the rose.

When the old woman died, her house was taken over by a miserly, disagreeable man, whose only real interest in life was making money. Barely a week had passed when he went out to the garden and ripped the tulips from the ground, replacing them with vegetables and clumps of parsley. This so angered the pixies that for years they crept out of the woods under the cloak of darkness to dance on the vegetables and tear at their roots. Of course, no plant could thrive under such an assault. Before long even the parsley leaves grew fringed and ragged, which is how you see them today.

At the same time the fairies took great pride in tending to the grave of the woman who had treated them so kindly. A thick carpet of grass flourished there, and at the head of the grave was a cluster of brightly colored tulips, each one blooming long after every other flower in the forest had died away. Sadly, in time other men moved in, and they, too, had no eye for beauty. The woods were cut down, the grave trampled, the stems of the tulips broken. The little people disappeared, taking refuge in the nearby hills. And ever since that time tulips have been smaller than they used to be, and less brightly colored. But saddest of all, gone is that sweet perfume that once hung in the air around Devonshire.

# THREE TREES BECOME EVERGREEN

(MONGOLIA)

*Most cultures have myths about sacred waters that allow either healing or immortality. Another Mongolian creation story tells how God fashioned models of the first man and woman out of clay, then left them for a time, guarded by a cat and dog. But in God's absence the Evil One came, bribed the cat and dog with milk and meat, then defiled the clay statues by urinating on them. When God returned, he placed drops of eternal water in the mouths of the models. They came alive all right, but because the Evil One had tainted them, the humans could never know immortality.*

IDDEN IN THE secret folds of the forest, nestled at the feet of great mountains where people rarely go, are the eternal springs—wells you may have sometimes heard referred to as fountains of youth. One day long ago a kindly swallow decided to share the gift of these precious waters with human beings, and by doing so, bring them immortality. So the good bird flew off to a spring in a secluded patch of woodland, scooped up a few drops of the magic water in his beak, and set out for the nearest village. And he nearly made it, too, but just outside the village a certain brutish bumble-bee, who had guessed the swallow's plan, flew up and stung the poor bird right on the belly.

Of course, this nasty sting hurt the swallow. As he groaned in pain, the drops of water spilled out from his beak onto three trees standing below: cedar, fir, and red bilberry. And that's why even today those trees remain evergreen, able to keep their leaves and needles through the whole year.

But there's yet another slice to serve from this story. Up until that time bumblebees were able to chortle the most pleasant, flutey songs, just like birds do. But that good swallow was so outraged by what had happened that he chased down the bee, caught it in his beak, and with a yank plucked out its tongue. And so while you can hear bumblebees buzz and mumble and hum, one thing you will never hear them do is sing. 🖛

# THE PEONY IS
# EXILED FROM THE
# ROYAL GARDEN

(CHINA)

*At the time Empress Wu-hou ruled China, it was considered
improper for commoners to cast glances toward a woman of
her stature, so she conducted public affairs of the state from
behind a curtain. Other tales tell of Wu-hou's penchant for
donning male dress—complete with false beard—and then
demanding that her court treat her as a man.*

WELVE HUNDRED YEARS AGO, during
the days of the Dragon Throne, the land was
ruled by a beautiful tyrant named Empress Wu-
hou. One winter night the Empress was loung-
ing in the royal chamber as she so often did, drinking wine,
fishing for compliments, boasting to her court ladies of her
many skills. In a rare quiet moment a breeze puffed through
the window, carrying with it the delightful scent of the plum
blossom. Being vain beyond reason, the Empress assumed
the plum had bloomed at will, for her pleasure alone. "It shall
be rewarded," she declared, and ordered one of the servants
to go out and adorn the tree with a beautiful red silk ribbon.
It's probably safe to say that the wine was kindling to her
vanity, for hardly had she polished off another glass when

she declared that surely the hundred flowers of the royal garden would also be blooming tonight, eager as they must be to please her.

But it was winter—the time of year when only the plum wears blooms—and when she got to the garden, not a single plant was in flower. The Empress was so angry she could hardly speak; despite their best efforts, none of her consorts could stem her rage. At one point she turned to the plants and threatened, "You will either be blooming by tomorrow or I shall see you punished!" And with that she stalked off, leaving the fairies in charge of the flowers trembling with fear. "It can't be done!" one of them cried. "Still," pointed out another, "we must try or be banished!" If only Peony, Queen of the Flowers, were here, they kept mumbling to themselves. But she had gone off for a night of games, and was nowhere to be found.

So it was that an astonishing mix of fairy snap and magic did induce the flowers to unfold that cold night, simply for the pleasure of the Empress. All, that is, except Peony, Queen of the Flowers. When the Empress walked to the garden in the morning and discovered the proud Peony still closed tight, she flew into another rage. Rousing the royal gardener from his bed, she ordered him to pull up every last peony plant—a lesson for all, she claimed, about the dangers of ingratitude.

That is how the peony was driven from the capital of Chang-an. It wasn't until long after the death of the pompous Empress Wu-hou that the Queen of Flowers braved her return.

# LOVERS IN THE BIRCH TREES

(PENOBSCOT INDIANS,
NORTHEASTERN UNITED STATES)
*Many stories of eastern Indian tribes contain a strong roman-
tic element—a sure sign of European influence. In the northeastern United States there was once a brisk trade of story
images between Native Americans and immigrants from
Europe, especially the French. As native nature stories gained
romance, American woodland tales sometimes embraced characters originating with the Indians.*

I T WAS HER FATE to live in a time when young
girls married men not of their choosing, but selected
for them by their parents or the chief. And while most
would have felt it a great honor to be paired with a
chief from another village, the sense of good fortune was
lost on her because she loved another. In the weeks after the
wedding she grew more and more despairing, and then sick-
ened. Day and night the people sat with her, offering their
prayers and soothing her brow, imploring her to reclaim her
life. Finally the conjure man was sent in the hopes that he
might heal her, but it wasn't possible, because she'd already
decided that death was the better place.

When she died it so broke the spirit of the man she loved
that he, too, grew sick and passed away. At his death the con-

jure man felt sorry, and so made a gift to the couple, turning them both into birch trees and standing them side by side in the cool of the forest. This is why when you walk the woods where the birch tree grows you'll find a pair of large trees standing together, and smaller ones clustered around, the children of lovers from long ago. ❧

# THE LEGEND OF THE SNOWDROP

(ENGLAND)

*The lovely snowdrop has long been prized in England, not just for its delicate bloom, but because it tends to blossom in the dreary days of February, when few other flowers can be found. An old belief says that if snowdrops are up by Candlemas, which falls on the second of February, it's a sign of good fortune for the coming year.*

O DOUBT YOU'VE HEARD much about that fateful day when Adam and Eve were turned out of the Garden of Eden. What you may not know is that the world they found outside that paradise was wrapped in the cold breath of winter; never before had either known any kind of discomfort, and suddenly there they were, adrift in a strange land of snow and wind and ice. Considering the trauma of such a transition, they did fairly well, quickly locating a cave to use as shelter from the bitter winds, learning to find food and make warm clothing from the skins of wild animals. But there was something that troubled Eve even more than the cold, a pain that no amount of heat from a fire or warm words from Adam could erase. It was the loss of the flowers that had once been her constant companions, the gentle blooms that laced the woods and meadows and stream banks of paradise.

One snowy day, desperate to catch even a glimpse of those

lost flowers, Eve crept back toward the gates of Eden. But no matter how carefully she approached, or from which direction, there stood the guardian angel, never allowing her close enough to see anything, not even to catch the smells of the blossoms carried in the breeze. Late in the day she finally gave up and turned for home, weeping. Now, the guardian angel who saw Eve in such pain felt a great sense of pity welling up inside. He stepped away from the gates, held out his hand, and caught one of the falling snowflakes. Then he raised his hand to his mouth and let go an easy breath, at which point the snowflake turned into a beautiful little flower. He presented it to Eve. "Let this bloom be a reminder that winter will not last forever," he told her, placing it in her palm. "Spring and then summer will roll across the earth, and when that happens, you will walk again with your beloved flowers."

It was the snowdrop the angel made that day, the snowdrop that brought new hope to that hopeless land.

# THE BIRTH OF THE ALMOND TREE

(TANGIER, MOROCCO)

*How the almond tree was created is one of many Islamic stories that celebrate the joys and miracles that can come to people who live with faith and generosity when they strive to put their lives in accord with the will of the Creator.*

HAT A BLESSING that through all of history there have been giving people, generous men and women with hearts as wide as the sky and brilliant as the sun. One among them was Princess Hatim, daughter of a sultan, who lived a time long before there was even such a thing as the land of Islam. Now, being the daughter of a sultan, Princess Hatim was of course wealthy beyond most people's grandest dreams, yet not a single dirham did she keep, preferring instead to give her riches to the poor. Though some members of her family thought her foolish, they never interfered; it was her wealth, after all, and she could do with it as she wished. But great trouble arose the day her father found out that in addition to giving away her own fortune, she'd also been giving away his.

Hatim had never mentioned this particular source of funding for her charities, nor did she show remorse when her father confronted her. "What would you suggest?" she asked, surprised that her father would be so upset. "Would you have me close my hand in the face of sickness and misery?" But her father saw the matter quite differently, as many no doubt would, and in the end he had to conclude that because his beloved Hatim had stolen from the royal family, she must be punished like any other. "You may choose death," he told her sadly, "or you may choose exile." After much anguish Hatim told her father she would take death. How could she, after all, a daughter of the Maghrib, ever survive in a place far away from her beloved homeland?

And so it was. But Allah was looking down from above that fateful day. Granting favor to Hatim for having been so generous, He decided to turn her into an almond, perhaps the finest of all the trees. How appropriate. To this day the almond tree continues to give gifts to the people: nuts and oil to help feed those who are hungry; and in spring, flowers so beautiful they bring joy to the troubled heart.

# THE CHANGING
# OF THE WARATAH
# BLOSSOM

(AUSTRALIA)

*It's from storytellers that aboriginal children in the outback of Australia first learn about the world—the wind and the rain, the plants and stars, indeed the very origins of the earth on which their people roam. These myths are vital links to the past, helping create in every new generation an unshakable sense of place. As it was done in the Dreamtime, children are often told, so we do it today.*

L ONG AGO IN THE MISTS of the Dreamtime there lived a great hunter named Wamili. Never before or since has there been a more skilled hunter, never a man whose spear flew so true, who so unfailingly kept his people supplied with bandicoots and emus and kangaroo. One dark, storm-ridden day when Wamili was out hunting, a flash of lightning ripped from the heavens and struck a tree, knocking him to the ground. Wamili's companion was nearby, and when he saw what had happened, he ran like the wind to reach his friend's side, all the while fearing him to be dead. But to his great surprise Wamili sat up, shook his head, in fact seemed to be in fine health. Yet when his friend suggested they return to camp, Wamili explained that for that he would need help. "You see, friend, I've been blinded. It's as if all the world is wrapped in the dark of night."

You might assume that a great hunter like Wamili would be utterly devastated to no longer be able to track game, to no longer be able to throw his spear and gather food for his people. But this was a man strong of heart, quick to see all the blessings that still remained. There was but one lingering sadness, and it had to do with the fact that he could no longer collect the food he prized above all the rest: the sweet, delicious nectar from the beautiful waratah tree. No matter that his touch was keen, it was impossible to tell the waratah blooms from those of other trees, many of which were poisonous. Wamili's wife, Kurita, was heartbroken to see her husband walking across the bush with hands outstretched, plant to plant, struggling to identify that one sweet pleasure. Unable to stand it any longer, one evening Kurita hurried out of camp to seek the aid of the tiny bush spirits, known as Kwinis. The Kwinis heard the heaviness in her heart; after talking briefly among themselves, they told her they would help, that they would stiffen the pistils of the waratah blossoms to make them more rigid than those of any other flower. In this way Wamili would be able to tell that he had indeed found the right plant.

And it was so. To the day he died Wamili wandered happily through the bush near his village, brushing his hand from blossom to blossom until it landed on the beautiful scarlet waratah, which he could identify with the slightest touch.

# COWSLIP AND THE KEYS OF HEAVEN

(ENGLAND)

*In early spring the yellow blooms of European cowslip—also known as keyflower, or keys of heaven—adorn woodlands and roadsides across much of England. For hundreds of years herbalists claimed that women could become more youthful looking simply by washing in water steeped with cowslip blossoms.*

S YOU PROBABLY KNOW, on the very day the good St. Peter was martyred, he was given the all-important job of gatekeeper at the kingdom of heaven. Maybe it was just that he was new and wanted to do a good job and all, but the truth is that at first he was terribly strict about who got into heaven and who ended up being turned away to that place called Limbo, designed for people not quite good enough for heaven but not quite bad enough for hell. Even people who were genuinely sorry for their sins were regularly turned away.

Now, this greatly distressed the angels; in fact, the day soon came when they just couldn't keep quiet any longer, so off they went to see Christ's mother, the Lady Mary. Mary listened carefully, as Mary always does, agreed that yes, this was certainly a problem, and promised each and every angel that she would personally take care of it. The next day when

St. Peter was fast asleep Mary crept up and unfastened the ring of golden keys from his belt. Then she walked over and not only unlocked the gates of heaven, but tossed those keys down through the clouds to earth so that heaven's gates could never be locked fast again. When the keys hit the ground, they blossomed into beautiful golden flowers— cowslips. The people of earth have prized them ever since, each spring finding them laced with the scent of heaven. As for St. Peter, he was rather ashamed of himself for having been so hard-hearted. Ever since, he's been much more forgiving, more willing to let people pass through those pearly gates into the bliss of paradise. ❧

# ALDER AND RHODODENDRON

(NEPAL)

*This tragic story of spurned love is from the rugged Himalayas of Nepal and has long been used to explain a small puzzle of nature: why the alder tree is found only in deep crevices and river bottoms.*

THOUGH IT MAY SEEM like a strange notion, there was a time many thousands of years ago when trees married—flowers, too— just like people do today. Of course, as often as not a good marriage takes a good matchmaker, and in this there was no one better than the stately fig. On a warm day in spring Fig was eyeing the forests of the foothills when he was struck by the incredible beauty of a red-flowered rhododendron. As was custom at the time, he sent word to the Goddess of the Forest, Bandevi, asking permission to begin looking for a suitable husband tree for the rhododendron, and Bandevi agreed.

Fig scouted the forest high and low, his eyes finally coming to rest on a handsome alder, tall of trunk and full of crown. The problem, it might be said, was that Alder was as fascinated by his own good looks as everyone else was. His response to Fig was rather sharp. "I suppose I can take a look at her," he said, "but not today. In my own good time." Well, Alder's own good time did not come until many months later, after Rhododendron had lost her green leaves and scarlet blossoms, and stood bare and crooked in the winter woods. Alder took one look, shook his head in disgust, and turned away.

Soon enough spring came again, and Fig went back to Alder to ask him to take one more look at Rhododendron. Alder was reluctant, but finally agreed. This time Rhododendron's beauty overwhelmed him—her dark green leaves, her cloak of scarlet flowers. "Of course I will marry her!" he cried to Fig. "Make the arrangements!"

And so Fig, excited at the prospect of making another fine match, went off to tell Rhododendron the news. "There will be no marriage," Rhododendron told him coolly. "Alder came last winter when I was bare of leaf and flower. Then I was not good enough for him. Understand that I cannot abide such a fickle heart."

When Alder heard of Rhododendron's rejection, he nearly doubled over with grief, so in love with her did he claim to be. One gray afternoon, sick with despair, he walked to the edge of the mountain and threw himself off, meeting his death at the bottom of a deep, dark ravine. Ever since then the alder has been found only in the cool, shadowy crevices that slice through the feet of the Himalayas. Soon after that sad day Bandevi, the Goddess of the Forest, declared that flowers and trees would marry no more.

# WALLFLOWER

(SCOTLAND)

*Wrapped in the fancy of this tale may be a grain of truth.*
*Some say there really was a young woman—Elizabeth,*
*daughter of the Earl of March—who fell in love with a boy*
*from an enemy clan. In this version she drops a wallflower*
*from the castle tower window as a signal to her lover that she's*
*ready to elope. Tragedy strikes, however, and on her way*
*down the wall she falls to her death. Her grief-stricken suitor*
*picks up the wallflower and affixes it to his cap, then leaves*
*Scotland, never to return.*

T HEY WERE WHAT could only be called star-crossed lovers: she the daughter of a great Scottish leader, head over heels in love with the son of her father's fiercest enemy. The two young people had been caught together once, and for the girl's father that was one time too many. From that day on she was never allowed to leave the castle except under guard—a prisoner, really, spending the bulk of her young life locked in a room at the very top of the castle tower. The boy argued and pleaded with his own family, begging them to understand the fire in his heart, but they would hear none of it. "Go near her," his father finally told him in a sour voice, "and I swear you'll regret you were born." But then what of such threats—what of jail or whipping or even death—in the face of true love?

One day the young man rose well before dawn, dressed himself in the clothes of a minstrel, and set off across the countryside to the home of his beloved. Of course, the guards at the castle saw him approach, but wandering minstrels were not at all uncommon in those days. After some joking and glad-handing with the guards, he persuaded them that there'd be no harm in letting him sit in the sun against the tower wall and while away the afternoon in song. "It will help pass the time," he assured them. "A little entertainment and the day will fly by." It took only minutes for his lover to come to the window, for she recognized his voice right away. For a long time he sang the old songs everyone knew, but eventually the guards lost interest and went back to talking among themselves, at which point the young man started singing an old tune but with very different words. His song told the story of a young man coming to elope with his lover at midnight; how he shot an arrow with a silk thread through her castle window, and how she pulled the thread up to reach a cord, which she wound up further to find a rope. This rope, the song continued, she tied to the bedpost, then she climbed down the wall and made off with her sweetheart into the night.

That same evening at midnight the young man crept back to the castle to find his beloved in the window waiting, dressed in her finest gown, looking so beautiful even in the faint light of a quarter moon that he lost his breath. He motioned for her to stand aside and then he shot that arrow through the window, just as the song described, with a silk thread tied to a cord, tied to a rope. But the one thing the song had not mentioned was how to affix that rope to the bedpost. No sooner had the maiden leaned out the window and begun her escape than the rope gave way, and she plunged to her death. The next morning, at each place she'd tumbled against the wall and spilled blood, there grew lovely scented flowers of gold and orange and russet—clusters of them, on tall stems. Even today the wild wallflower still prefers to hug the stones of buildings and garden walls, a reminder of that sad day in Scotland long ago.

# LEGEND OF THE AZALEA

(CHINA)

*Here again we see death giving birth to exquisite new life, this time in the form of a beautiful flower. The idea that drops of blood can foster new flowers or trees is a common one, and to some degree it may be based upon actual experiences. There were many claims in historical times, for example, of roses springing up on blood-soaked battlefields. In ninth-century Spain, a rose sprang up on a mountain pass where a horrific battle—which claimed the lives of Charlemagne's nephew Roland and two dozen knights—took place. Ever since that time, the Spanish name for this flower has been* firo dei escarmujo, *or "the flower of the skirmish."*

 HOULD YOU EVER be lucky enough to find yourself wrapped in the glory of a China spring, you may wonder at the sad, plaintive cry of the little cuckoo: To sing such a sad song in the midst of such beauty! What kind of tragedy could have led to this?

A long time ago there lived a widow who was mother to two fine boys, the younger being her own child, and the elder, a stepson. What shadow filled this woman's heart no one can say, but while she fawned over her own child, treating him like a prince with fine food and the best of clothes, to her stepson she was mean and full of contempt. The older boy's world was a place of hard labor and scant rations and terrible, hateful beatings. Yet between the brothers there was great fondness. The younger one always made it a point to do whatever he could to make the older boy's life a little easier: stealing food from the kitchen and taking it to him as he sweated in the fields, for example, or willingly taking the blame for whatever mistakes the elder brother might have made.

One spring day the mother hatched an evil plan. "Take these two bags of seeds and plant them in the fields," she told the boys. "But be advised of this. Should one of the bags of seed not take, then that boy need not return to this house, for I will have disowned him forever." In truth the seeds given to her stepson had been roasted on the stove and had no chance of ever sprouting. What she couldn't foresee, though, was that her cherished younger child suspected foul play and switched bags with his older brother. Now, the younger boy knew his mother would meet such trickery—even by her favored son—with terrible anger, would in fact give him a sound beating. To save himself from such a fate, on the day he noticed his brother's seeds were sprouting and his were not, he waited until the middle of the night when everyone was asleep, then packed some clothes and ran away into the hills.

Furious that her plan had been so thoroughly undone, the widow took her rage out on the older boy, whipping him until he could barely stand. "Get out of this house and find your brother!" she cried. "And should you fail, wretch, rest assured that this is the last spring you'll ever see!" So off he went, sobbing, searching high and low for his precious brother. "Ti-ti, where have you gone?" he cried. "Please come back, Ti-ti." Looking down from above, the gods were greatly saddened by such a pitiful sight; that afternoon they changed the poor boy into a cuckoo, giving him wings to help him on his search. It's the sad cry of that weary boy that you hear in the cuckoo's voice today.

By late summer he was too weary to look any further, so he sat on a branch at the edge of the woods and wept until he had no more tears to give. What fell from his eyes then were a few tiny drops of blood, and with that the little-boy-turned-bird sighed and passed away. From those drops of blood on the ground there arose the most beautiful red flower—an azalea—memorial to the great love between that boy and his lost brother. ❧

# CREATURES

# GREAT

## *and*

# SMALL

# THE BIRDS FIND
# THEIR HOMES

*This story of how the birds found their homes comes from Luba country, a vast, stirring reach of wooded savanna between the Lomami and Zaire rivers. Like so many African tales, this one is typically told in song, the audience joining in on the refrain, becoming the voice of the mother bird. The song is a wonderful slice of nature lore, teaching listeners the habitats of many birds.*

 LONG TIME AGO there was a powerful bird who lived on a wide, grassy plain, and no one knew her name. From this bird came a great many children—so many, in fact, that the day came when they could no longer find enough food. So the bird called her family together to tell them they would have to leave the plain in search of more abundant lands. The children gathered around their mother and took hold of her feathers, and with great sweeps of her wings she carried them into the sky.

She flew for many miles, searching, and in time some of the children holding on to her feathers grew tired. The hummingbird looked down and spotted gardens of beautiful red flowers; "I will remain here," she said, and let go of her mother to settle in this new place. Awhile later the little black kokodyo spotted fruit trees on the ground below and announced that he, too, had reached the end of his journey. And on it went. The weaver bird chose fields of bran and the desert pelican patches of wild olives; the pepper bird found his home in a big forest, while the secretary bird settled next to the termites. In time all found new homes—the crested crane and the pigeon, the water bird and the wild goose and the honey bird. Homes where they could bear children of their own.

When the mother bird saw that none of her children were left, she climbed high in the sky and soared for hours in great circles. Today this bird has the respect of all the people. They know her as Eagle Who Announces the Drought, a name that refers to her habit of foretelling the short dry spell that occurs in the middle of the Luba rainy season.

That is how all the birds came to be, from the womb of one bird who laid her eggs on the plain.

# WHY SPIDER HAS A SMALL WAIST

(LIBERIA)

*When parents in western Africa want to teach their children
the consequences of being greedy, there's nothing better than a
spider story. Spider is clever, to be sure—a trickster in the best
tradition. But his habit of always wanting far more than he
needs usually lands him in trouble.*

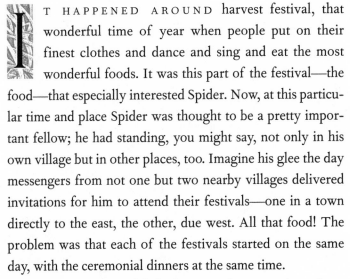

IT HAPPENED AROUND harvest festival, that
wonderful time of year when people put on their
finest clothes and dance and sing and eat the most
wonderful foods. It was this part of the festival—the
food—that especially interested Spider. Now, at this particular time and place Spider was thought to be a pretty important fellow; he had standing, you might say, not only in his
own village but in other places, too. Imagine his glee the day
messengers from not one but two nearby villages delivered
invitations for him to attend their festivals—one in a town
directly to the east, the other, due west. All that food! The
problem was that each of the festivals started on the same
day, with the ceremonial dinners at the same time.

After plenty of careful thinking, Spider secured two long
pieces of stout rope and tied one end of each around his
waist. Then he convinced a friend to take the loose end of
the ropes to each of the villages. "Find me men who are
strong and reliable," he said. "Tell them just before the feast-

ing begins that they should give a hard yank on the rope. I'll run over as fast as I can and join them." Now, as I said, Spider had already been told that both feasts would begin at the same time, but he was counting on the inevitable delays that surround such celebrations to give him an hour or so leeway. Plenty of time for eating at both places.

The day of the festival arrived, and there Spider sat, halfway between the two villages, two ropes tied fast around his waist, waiting. Much to his dismay, when the sun reached that certain place in the sky, he felt both ropes go tight at once. Of course, being pulled hard in two directions, he couldn't move at all. Who knows exactly how long he stood there struggling, not going anywhere. But it was plenty long enough to make him miss not one feast, but both! To make matters worse, his friend had given the rope ends to a couple of very strong young men, just as he'd been instructed. All that vigorous pulling on Spider's waist squeezed it down to a small fraction of what it was before, and that is why the spider has such a small waist. ✕

# NANABOZHO AND THE WILD GEESE

(OJIBWA INDIANS, NORTH-CENTRAL
UNITED STATES AND CENTRAL CANADA)

*Along the Canadian shore of Lake Superior is a low rock
promontory that looks a great deal like a slumbering giant.
Indeed, this is the great Nanabozho of the Ojibwa people—
creator, magician, and almost endless source of wisdom,
trickery, and foolishness. Much of the look and feel of the
north woods, from lakes to birch trees to primitive rock art on
granite cliffs, can be attributed to the amazing feats of
Nanabozho.*

 HEN NANABOZHO was young he spent
his days like many boys and girls of the far
north, exploring the wooded nooks and
creeks and shimmering lakes of the region.
One bright autumn day while out picking berries, he happened to hear the sound of an enormous flock of wild geese
coming in from the north, looking for a stopover place as
they hurried to escape the cold slap of winter. By watching
carefully, Nanabozho was able to follow them to a large,
rock-bound lake where they settled down to feed and rest
until morning. Just the sight of them made Nanabozho's
mouth water, for if there was one thing he loved, it was a
wild-goose dinner roasted over a crackling fire.

But it wasn't enough just to jump out from the bushes and

grab two or three of the geese as they scattered. No, his was an appetite that would require more than that. Returning to the forest, Nanabozho stripped off lengths of cedar bark from the trees and braided them into a long, strong rope. Coiling this line in his hand, he took a big breath and dove under the water, swam to where the geese were resting, then quietly but quickly set about tying a knot around the foot of one bird after another. He could have stopped after a dozen or so, mind you, because that would have been plenty for dinner. But that wasn't Nanabozho's way. Determined to get every last goose, he was eventually forced up for breath, at which point several of the birds spotted him and sounded the alarm. In the wink of an eye the flock was flapping their great wings and rising into the air, dragging Nanabozho with them! On and on they flew, trailing the great giant behind, until finally they crossed over a patch of wet ground and Nanabozho let loose, dropping into the swamp, where he landed on his bottom with a great, squishy thud. To hear him tell the story, it was as if all of this had been carefully planned—as if the entire escapade was just a scheme to see what it might feel like to fly through the air like a bird. And who among us is going to argue with a giant?

There was a curious, rather unexpected side effect to Nanabozho's adventure, however. Remember how those geese were all tied together with that rope of braided cedar bark? That meant the strongest bird of the flock ended up pulling all the others along through the air, in the process forming a shape that looked very much like the letter V. And as you know, migrating geese have been flying that same formation ever since. 🦅

# A TALE OF SKYLARK

(JAPAN)

*One colony of skylarks exists in North America, located in the pastures of southern Vancouver Island. Skylarks routinely climb in long spirals many hundreds of feet in the air; from those heights they utter a thin chortle for several minutes, then make a fast plunge back to earth.*

HEN THE UPPER and lower worlds were first made, Skylark was among those privileged creatures allowed to remain in the far reaches of heaven, close by the Creator's side. One morning the Creator needed to send word of some important matter to the spirits living down in Ainuland, and chose Skylark as His messenger. "Remember this one thing," the Creator said to Skylark. "Return to heaven before the fall of night."

So Skylark wheeled down from the heavens in that beautiful spiral dance of hers, finally reaching Ainuland, where she delivered the Creator's message. While there Skylark grew enchanted with the beauty of earth—the flowers and the waterfalls, the mountains and forests and the rumble of waves along the seashore. So busy was she exploring that she forgot all about the Creator's instructions to return before dark, and ended up spending the night here on earth. The next morning at dawn she began her spiral dance back to the heavens, but when she reached a height of some five or six hundred feet, she could go no higher, for the Creator, upset by her disobedience, had shut the doors of heaven and would not permit her to return.

It was then that Skylark began to protest in that thin, chortling voice we've come to know, arguing that surely she shouldn't be punished simply for being overwhelmed by the staggering beauty of things made by the Creator. All to no avail. Even now, every day Skylark climbs to a point high in the sky where she argues her case to be let back into heaven. So far the Creator has refused her, and after a time, tired of flying and weary from debate, she plunges back to earth.

# HOMAGE
# TO THE ANTS

(BURMA)

*Small creatures often triumph over stronger ones, through either wisdom or providence. In this tale, the tiny ant—so often overlooked—secures a remarkable special privilege as payment for poor treatment at the paws of the king.*

OT LONG AFTER LION first assumed his role as ruler of the jungle, all the creatures came to pay respects to the king of the beasts. It was a glorious day full of pomp, and all the animals arrived looking their best, every paw washed, every inch of fur and feathers preened. On the ground among the crowd, all but unnoticed, was the humble ant, who in fact had traveled a very long way just for the chance to bow before the king. Much to Ant's dismay, when the time came for him to approach the royal throne, the other animals, even the lion, scoffed at him and brushed him off as if he were unfit for such an important occasion.

Now, when word of this incident reached the king of the ants, he was furious—so angry, in fact, that that very night he summoned a worm and told him to slip over to the palace and crawl into the ear of the lion as he slept. Lion awoke the next morning in terrible pain, roaring like thunder, a commotion that naturally brought all the other animals running from their beds. But no matter how hard they tried, none of them—not Snake and not Turtle, not Rabbit and not Leopard—could get at the tiny worm. By evening the entire camp was beside itself, and the great king lion knew what he must do. Gulping down his pride, he traveled through the woods to the king of ants and groveled at his feet—stumbled all over himself, in fact, making apologies for having scoffed at the humble ant who'd come to call at his coronation. The ruling ant left the lion to stew only a little while before calling over one of his servants and instructing him to crawl into the lion's ear and pluck out the worm.

Not long after this the world was divided, and all the animals were given territories in which to live—homes that each has kept to this very day. But not the ants. As partial payment for the wrong done to them, ants were allowed to come and go where they pleased: on the ground and in trees, on the rocks and bushes, even in people's homes—kitchens and attics and pantries and parlors. And no king, no matter how mighty, has ever dared scoff at them again.

# WREN BECOMES KING OF THE BIRDS

(IRELAND)

*Most of us have a special fondness for myths about animals with exceptional strength, beauty, or wisdom. Thus, the perceived cleverness of the wren has been celebrated in stories for thousands of years.*

I T WAS IN THE DAYS of curiosity—a time when all the creatures of earth were exploring their abilities, mapping out the boundaries of their world—that the birds came together to select an able ruler, someone who could be counted on to look after their interests in the years to come. There were robins and hawks, eagles and doves, sandpipers and pelicans, falcons and curlews and jays, flycatchers and sparrows, chickadees, ducks, and dippers. Some suggested electing a leader based on the colorfulness of his plumage or on who possessed the greatest speed, while others said it should be left to him with the most beautiful song. Eventually it was decided that whoever among them could fly the highest would win the right to lead the others. Such a show of strength, they reasoned, would be worth a great deal in meeting the challenges of difficult times.

Now, of course, such a contest favored the more powerful birds, and it was quite a site on that day watching Hawk and Falcon and Eagle preening their feathers, stretching their necks, readying their wings for the long climb into the heavens. With all that going on, it's no surprise that the tiny wren could have gone unnoticed when at the last minute he crept up and nestled himself between the great mat of brown feathers on Eagle's back.

Robin blew the whistle, and off the contestants flew, spiraling ever higher, until the earth lay far below. On they climbed for five days and nights, until finally only the eagle and the hawk remained to soar in that thin, cold air. At last the hawk's wings gave out, too, and only the eagle could reach any higher. "It's finished," Eagle cried out. "Of all who fly, I've come the highest." The birds below were awestruck by his terrific strength, certain they'd made a wise choice in rulers.

Then, just as the eagle began to drop back to earth, the tiny wren crawled out from between his feathers and leapt free. Being well rested, of course, Wren was able to flutter even higher than Eagle had gone, dancing and spinning as though it was just another morning trip over the meadows. "Look here," Wren called down to Eagle. "See that it's me who climbs the highest of all the birds!" Eagle could hardly believe his eyes. But fair is fair, and he never was a poor loser. "Behold!" Eagle called down to the other birds. "Wren is our new king!"

And all the other birds were quick to give Wren his due. They figured that no matter how he might have pulled off such a feat, it must have taken a great deal of cleverness. And cleverness wasn't a bad thing to have in difficult times. ➤

# TSENZI,
# THE HONEY BIRD

(ZIMBABWE)

*The honey bird takes its name from a curious habit it has of
calling sharply to passersby, then leading them, tree by tree,
to the location of a beehive. When native people find honey
by such means, they always leave a piece of the comb for the
bird to eat. Fail to do so, an old saying has it, and the next
time Tsenzi may lead you to a lion!*

T HERE IS LITTLE that Tsenzi, the honey
bird, loves to do more than eat. One day from
his perch high up in a tree he saw in the distance
an elephant lying dead on the ground. What an
abundance of food for a bird! Tsenzi wasted no time flying
over to the elephant to claim it as his own, as one must do
when seeking such a prize. But just when the honey bird was
congratulating himself for the find of the season, who
should pop out from behind the elephant's head but a shrew
mouse by the name of Dune? "Not so fast," said the mouse.
"Had you been paying attention, you would have seen that I
arrived here first. This elephant is all mine." The mouse then
pointed to a scrape in the sand, claiming it to be his nest.
Tsenzi, however, who never missed much, knew that the
mouse had hurriedly scooped out the sand with his tail just
seconds before.

The mouse and the honey bird argued over the elephant

for the rest of the afternoon, until both nearly lost their voices from the effort. Finally Dune had an idea. "Let's take our case to the bees," he suggested. And Tsenzi agreed. The bees listened carefully to both parties, buzzed about for a time, then delivered their verdict. The elephant, they said, belongs to Dune. Now, while Tsenzi had in fact agreed to let the bees decide, he was still angry; to his way of thinking, those bees had acted hastily. He knew full well that Dune had lied about having his nest there beside the elephant's head. Wasn't that proof enough that he couldn't be trusted? Poor Tsenzi. He never got over it. That's why to this day the honey bird goes out of his way to catch the attention of a man or woman passing by, then leads them on to rob the nearest beehive.

It may seem strange that a bird would hold such bad feelings for so long, but consider this. People say if you listen carefully to the bees in southern Zimbabwe, you can hear them buzzing this same taunting phrase over and over: "Nzou nde ya dune"—the elephant belongs to Dune.

# WHY BAT HANGS UPSIDE DOWN

(LAKE ALBERT, THE CONGO)
*No character fault is highlighted more often in nature stories than greed. Here, the greedy party, Lightning, isn't so much punished directly (how, after all, would one go about punishing lightning?), but rather is spurned for all time by Bat, one of the wisest and most respected of the animals.*

A LONG TIME AGO when Bat was king of his country, he and his wife and many children came and went with all the pomp and prestige that royalty affords. His kraals were filled with goats and cows, his food baskets overflowed, and as for his chickens, well, who could even begin to count them? In the evenings the cooks prepared fine, rich dishes for the family, all with one kind of meat or another, which is in itself testimony to just how wealthy Bat really was.

One day while out surveying his kingdom, Bat was hailed by a strange voice. It was Lightning, king of another realm high above the earth, who'd come to propose that the two rulers draw up a treaty of kinship, a pact of blood-brotherhood to ensure peaceful relations for all times. Well, Bat was a lover of peace and good intention, and such a gesture moved him. He ordered his cooks to prepare the grandest of feasts for his guest, and by that evening the tables in his house were heavy with dishes that most people would think themselves fortunate even to dream about. Partway through dinner Lightning's gaze fell on a beautiful serving platter, a royal heirloom handed down to Bat from a long line of ancestors. "I tell you, my friend," Lightning said, "that platter is the most stunning thing I've ever seen. I simply must have it." Bat made a sweeping gesture, pointing to all the fine things that filled his home. "Take anything else you see, my friend, but that platter is part of the royal house. Truly, it is not mine to give."

Of course, most people would have understood such a thing, how some possessions are simply beyond giving away. But not Lightning. He took Bat's refusal as a great insult, and demanded that Bat turn the platter over at once! When Bat refused, Lightning stomped out of the house and rose to the sky, where he sent down fierce bolts of fire. In a matter of minutes Bat's house and all that he owned were destroyed.

Bat stood heartbroken beside the ashes, grief-stricken by the loss of his home, of his chickens and cows and goats. And when the grief ripened and fell away, Bat was left with only anger and contempt for Lightning's greedy ways. It was then that King Bat made his famous declaration. From that moment on he and his children and all their offspring would turn their backs to the sky, would hang beneath trees and from the roofs of caves, facing earth—a sign of their great displeasure at Lightning's awful behavior. ➴

# MEADOWLARK
# GAINS HIS VOICE

(POMO INDIANS, NORTH-CENTRAL CALIFORNIA)
*Pomo cultures associate all four of the animals mentioned
in this story with the underworld. Meadowlark is known as
the destroyer, his role being to dismantle the physical world
so that the parts can be used over and over, and the spirit
born again.*

IT'S COMMON KNOWLEDGE that of all the birds
of the world, Meadowlark is among the most accomplished singers; many a farmer and rancher, walker
and wanderer have stopped beside some fence post in
the sweet thick of spring to savor his repertoire of warbles
and trills and twitters. But it wasn't always this way. In fact,
there was a time when Meadowlark had a rather plain, unre-
markable voice, as unlikely to catch your attention as the
cluck of a hen or the squawk of a jay. But that was before the
contest.

It happened out in the forest long ago, when Meadowlark,
Chicken Hawk, Ground Squirrel, and Buzzard were all talking together in a fevered pitch, each one trying to make a
point, creating such a clatter that not one of them could hear
the others. At the time it was Buzzard, not Meadowlark, that
had the beautiful voice; even in that heated argument you
could hear the lilt of it, rising and falling like someone playing scales on a bamboo flute. Finally Chicken Hawk jumped

up and down, waving his wings to get everyone's attention; his friends fell silent. "This babbling is getting us nowhere!" he said. "I've got an idea. Let's pair up and have a contest to see who can keep silent the longest!" After much talk it was decided that the winning side would be able to speak in the languages of all the others.

"And what for the losers?" said Buzzard in that musical voice of his. The losers, it was concluded, would remain silent forever. Sides were chosen: Meadowlark and Ground Squirrel would go up against Buzzard and Chicken Hawk.

And so the contest began. Before long all the animals of the forest were gathered round—not just to watch, mind you, but to make all manner of jokes and smart remarks, trying to get the four friends to start laughing. Well, the breaking point came thanks to Ku-all, the night owl, who said something that started a roll of laughter deep down in Buzzard's belly. Oh, he tried to squelch it, all right, closing his beak and hiding his head under his wing, but it was like trying to hold back a volcano or an ocean wave. When he finally opened his beak to laugh, not a sound was heard. Buzzard had lost his beautiful voice. His partner, Chicken Hawk, was hardly any better off, able to utter nothing but a raspy whistle.

It was then that Meadowlark opened his beak and began to sing, filling the woods not only with his own voice, but with the languages of his three friends. To this day the people say that Meadowlark has four voices. And poor Buzzard, once the grandest singer, has no song at all. ➤

# SAD CROAK OF THE GREEN FROG

(KOREA)

*Surely it wouldn't take more than one summer evening in the rain, listening to the low, slow croak of green frogs, to weave a sad story like this one. Wrapped up in this mournful image, though, is an ancient moral about the need for children to treat their parents with respect.*

ONE EXPECTS SOME measure of contrariness in the young, yet sometimes there comes one so stubborn that he drives his poor mother to distraction—someone like a certain green frog who lived long ago. No matter what his mother asked him to do, the frog did the opposite: Told to go on an errand in the mountains, he went instead to the river; reminded that it was time for silence, he instead would talk and sing. When Frog was still fairly young, his mother became ill. Over the months she grew steadily worse, until one day death appeared on the near horizon. All her adult life this woman had wanted to be buried in the mountains, where the air was bright with sun, but how to make certain her request would be carried out with such a contrary son in charge of things? Then she had an idea. From her sickbed she beckoned her son. "Whatever you do," she pleaded, "don't bury me on the mountain. It's the river where I wish to lay. Do you understand? The river."

When his mother finally died, Green Frog felt terrible. How cruel he'd been to her all those years! How could he live with himself under such a blanket of shame? Deciding then and there to turn over a new leaf, Frog recalled his mother's last wish: to be buried by the river. So down to the river he went to prepare a place. The problem with such a location, of course, was that whenever it rained, the river rose; many a sleepless night did Green Frog have in such weather, sitting on the shore with a worried look on his face, wondering whether this would be the time his mother's grave would wash away. It was during these dreadful vigils that Frog began lamenting in a low, sad voice—season after season, year after year. That's why even today when the clouds pour rain, the frog lets out a dejected-sounding croak, exactly as his cousin did long ago. ➤

# THE ORIGIN OF
# BUTTERFLIES

(KOREA)

*Linking the birth of butterflies to someone dying in the throes*
*of grief is a powerful image, suggesting that those who suffer*
*on earth will find freedom and release in the hereafter.*

T'S WISE TO remember that when death comes in
the front door, new life is already standing out back;
that out of tragedy are sometimes born small miracles. Which is precisely what happened when a poor
young girl of long ago, soon to be married to a man she'd
not yet met, had death take him just weeks before the wedding. Every day thereafter this young girl would dress in her
palanquin of many colors, drape the white mourning cloth
about her, then go to the man's house and weep. So too each
day, morning and evening, did she go to the grave and cry
his name.

How is it, you might wonder, that a young girl should
mourn so for a man she never met? But you must understand that this happened in a time when the daughter of
a gentleman, once married or betrothed, did not marry
again. This tragedy, therefore, wasn't only a matter of
someone having lost her future partner, but losing much of
her own life as well. Every day the girl would go to the
grave and cry out how she was ready to meet her fiancé
in the spirit place; she would pray that if they were truly

kindred, the grave would open and take her, let her cross to the other side.

One morning she made her way to the grave as usual, accompanied by an elderly house maid. This time, though, at the sound of those prayers, the grave really did open up, and the girl jumped in. Terrifying as such a sight was, the maid rushed over and made a desperate grab for her mistress. But in the end she came away with nothing but a shred of the girl's skirt.

As the maid stood there, shocked, staring at the closing grave, the skirt fabric started breaking into pieces and falling from her hands. Before a single scrap could reach the ground, though, it turned into a beautiful butterfly and quietly flew away. The colors and patterns you see on butterfly wings today are the colors and patterns from that poor girl's skirt. ➤

# SACRED GOOSE GETS HIS GOLDEN BREAST

(TIBET)

*Footraces between a fast creature and a slow but more clever one is a common theme in nature stories around the world. In Zimbabwe, for example, the competition occurs between an antelope and a tortoise; the tortoise ends up winning, using the very same ruse employed by this frog from Tibet.*

IDDEN AMONG THE great mountains of Tibet is a little-known peak, its summit flat as a table and covered with gardens of grass and long runs of wildflowers. From the beginning of time this has been a favorite place of creatures of all kinds—somewhere to run with the winds, a perch from which to gaze into the far reaches of the world. A long time ago Frog and Rabbit were up on this very mountain, playing as good friends will do on summer days, when what should they stumble across but a pot filled with gold! Frog was first to shout out a claim. "What a fortune I've found! Who would have imagined I'd be so lucky!" But Rabbit would hear none of that. "It's mine!" he yelled, in a voice so loud and harsh it made Frog shudder. "I saw it before you did!" Thus began a terrible fight, which went on well into the afternoon. Finally exhausted, Rabbit called a time-out. "Look, Frog," he panted, "this is getting us nowhere. I say we go back down to the foot of the mountain, and tomorrow morning at dawn we'll race back to this very spot. The winner takes the pot of gold."

Well, you might think such a plan ludicrous given the speed at which rabbits can run, but the fact is Frog readily agreed that this would be the perfect way to decide the matter. When they parted company, Rabbit made for home, but Frog hopped to the home of his two cousins, both of whom looked exactly like him. Promising to pay them handsomely for their efforts, he escorted one to a point about halfway up the mountain and told him to wait there until the next day, and to hop like mad for the summit at the first sign of Rabbit's approach. He took his other cousin to the top and told him to sit on the pot of gold. The race began right on schedule, at dawn. Rabbit, who was hopping along at a good clip, was downright astonished to get halfway up the mountain only to find Frog leaping wildly ahead of him. Showing great determination, Rabbit hopped faster, and then even faster still, the head wind from his speedy run laying his ears flat against his back. Yet when he reached the top, there was Frog sitting on top of the pot of gold. He'd lost the race!

Even though Frog claimed victory, his troubles were just beginning. The sad truth was that try as he might, there was no way in the world he could get that gold down the mountain. As he sat there puzzling over the problem, a large goose—dark in color with a brownish breast—flew by, spotted Frog, and stopped to ask what the trouble was. Frog explained the problem and then, seeing how big and strong Goose was, asked if he'd consider carrying the pot down the mountain. "I will be happy to," replied Goose. "But for my efforts I'd very much like half the gold." Well, what could Frog do but agree?

After the treasure had been divided and the two had gone their separate ways, Goose sat for a long time, marveling at the sheer beauty of the gold. In the end he decided to take his half and rub it into his feathers from neck to belly, turning his breast into that beautiful color we see today. This coloring is sacred to the people of Tibet, and so they show great reverence for this beautiful bird of the high country, which by the way is very tame, showing little fear of humans. Many claim these geese, known as Ngamg-ba, are reincarnations of holy men, are the new lives taken by priests who once prayed from these same glorious mountains.

# WHY THE ROBIN HAS A RED BREAST

(IRELAND)

*The robin has a special place in the hearts of the Irish, who celebrate him with numerous stories of how he came by his beautiful red breast. Pester or injure this bird, and you flirt with bad luck. In Ireland boys were warned by their parents to stay away from birds' nests—especially those of the robin; steal the eggs, they cautioned, and you'll have sore hands for days.*

IT WAS IN A TIME now all but lost, a season ground to dust and scattered by the winds. In those days all of humankind held only one fire, and the job of caring for it had fallen to one old man and a young boy. One would rest while the other sat on the ground beside the flames, carefully feeding pieces of wood whenever the blaze began to weaken.

One day during his watch the boy grew weary, and while meaning only to rest his eyes for a moment, fell fast asleep. As it happened, a wolf was watching from just inside the woods. When he saw the boy sleeping, he hurried out, turned his back to the flames, and set about kicking dirt with his hind legs until the fire sputtered, paused, and then flickered out. And still the boy slept on.

Of course, that could well have been the end of it, and who can guess the years that might have passed before humans managed another such chance at holding flame? Luckily, however, on that particular day, unseen by either boy or wolf, was a robin watching from a bush beside the fire. No sooner had the wolf gone back into the woods than the bird hopped out, and finding a single red spark, started flapping his wings as fast as he could in hopes of fanning that one lone ember back to life. Sure enough, the spark turned to a flicker, the flicker to a flame, the flame to a blaze. In fact, the blaze grew so big that it singed the robin's breast, searing it to that rusty color we see today. ➤

# TALES

## *from*

## *the*

# HEAVENS

# SILVER RIVER

(VIETNAM)

*That beautiful stream of silky light we call the Milky Way is known in Vietnam as the Silver River. Of all the tales that have sprouted from its banks, none is more full of joy and sorrow than the story of two lovers, Ngau Lang and Chuc Nu.*

**T**HERE IS IN every world and every time beings of great beauty, and in the heavenly empire of long ago none was more fair than young Chuc Nu, the Sacred Spinner. Each day would find her hard at work spinning the yarns of heaven on the grassy banks of the Silver River. One day the Sacred Shepherd, a strong and handsome man named Ngau Lang, was out drifting with his flock when he came upon Nu. The two young people talked and laughed the day away while they worked, trading stories as the river lapped against its banks. The next day Lang returned and again they shared company, and again the day after that, until after several weeks both felt the fire of a great love. The Emperor of the Heavens could see that love clearly when the couple came to ask his permission to marry, and he was only too happy to give his blessing. "There is one condition," he told them. "Both of you have important work to do, spinning yarn and tending the flocks, and that work must go on without fail." The couple readily agreed, and then they were off, back to the banks of the Silver River.

Maybe you can understand how a pair of young lovers might forget promises and commitments, forget all of life's obligations in the face of their delight. Well, that is just what happened to Nu and Lang. They were so busy being together—lying in the sun and finding flowers on the grassy hills, swimming and fishing in the Silver River—that the sheep went untended, the yarn unspun.

When the Emperor of the Heavens heard about this, he was furious, and sent word demanding that Lang and Nu come to the palace at once. "You have disobeyed the one condition of your coupling," he scolded. "Your punishment will be your parting. From this day on, Lang, you will tend your flocks on one side of the Silver River, and Nu, you will spin on the other. Each year I will call the ravens of earth to flock here and form a bridge for you to cross; you will then have a single month to share together."

And with that Lang and Nu were dismissed, to begin the next eleven months on opposite sides of the Silver River. So heartbroken were they that each wept, their grief so great that tears began to pool and fall as rain in Vietnam. Ever since then in summer Lang and Nu come together with great joy for one entire month, but in parting they grieve again, their tears lasting for several months, pooling and falling to earth.

And that is why each year, from July until October, there is a rainy season in Vietnam. ✳

# BIRTH OF THE SUN

(AUSTRALIA)

*In addition to storytelling, Australia's aborigines also share the essence of tribal history through musical chants, which are also sometimes used as prayers to influence the processes of nature. Important myths are often depicted through various kinds of paintings and decorations, as well as by elaborate theatrical presentations.*

I T WAS A TIME when the world was a dark, cool place, not yet bathed in the bright rays of the sun. Birds flew, kangaroos ran, people hunted and gathered their meals in the shadows, guided only by the pale light of the moon. Brolga and Emu sat on their nests under a sliver of moon, each one boasting, as those two tended to do, about how her children were the most beautiful in the land. What started as a mild squabble soon turned into a screeching frenzy, each hurling insults at the other. After one particularly nasty comment, Brolga ran over to Emu's nest, plucked one of the eggs out with her bill, and with a violent shake of her head hurled it into the sky. As chance would have it, that egg smashed right into the middle of a huge pile of sticks gathered by the sky people; on impact it burst into flame, then grew into an enormous bonfire, lighting the world below, revealing its true beauty for the very first time.

Seeing this, the sky people decided that those on earth

should have light more often, so they decided to create the cycle of night and day. From then on each night a pile of wood was collected and at first sign of the morning star, one of the sky people set it afire. At first the fire burns small, bathing the world in the weak light of morning, but by midday the entire woodpile is burning and the land below is hot and bright; by evening the fire calms to embers, then fades away entirely, making way for night.

The trouble was that on cloudy days no one could see the morning star. The fire went unlit, and the world below remained as it had been before, wrapped in darkness. After much discussion the sky people solved the problem with the help of the kookaburra bird. Every morning the kookaburra sings at the top of his lungs, calling out in peals of what sounds like rollicking laughter, letting the sky people know that the time has come again to spark the pile of wood and light the world. ✪

# FROG AND THE MARRIAGE OF SUN AND MOON'S DAUGHTER

(ANGOLA)

*This "Jacob's Ladder"–style story from the Angola Bantu was first recorded nearly one hundred years ago. One curious feature of the tale is that here Moon has been cast as Sun's wife; in most other Bantu myths, Moon is a male, married to the morning and evening stars.*

IS NAME WAS KIMANUELE. Not only was he handsome, this young son of a great chief, but he was filled with a resolve unknown to most men. One evening, soon after Kimanuele had passed into manhood, his father sat down with him and asked his thoughts on marriage. "Oh, I've been thinking about it," Kimanuele confessed. "The truth is, Father, there's only one woman for me. She is the daughter of Sun and Moon." Kimanuele's father, himself a man of great vision, was nearly dumbstruck by such a confession. And yet he did nothing to discourage the boy. "You must write a letter to Sun and Moon," he told his son. "In the meantime, I'll try my best to find someone to deliver it."

That was the hard part. Not a single one of the dozens of

birds and animals summoned by the chief was able to help, but just as he was about to give up, in hopped Minuti, the wise old frog. "I can deliver your letter," he said matter-of-factly, in that cool, unflapping way frogs have of talking. And with that the chief handed his son's letter to the frog and off he hopped, making his way to a quiet, hidden pond that few humans even knew existed. That night, like most nights, a long golden cord spun by thousands of spiders dropped from the sky, down which came two sky maidens, who set about filling enormous clay jugs with drinking water from the pond. At the last minute Minuti slipped into one of those jugs; the vessels were hauled up into the heavens and placed atop a massive table in the corner of Sun's chambers. Peering around to make sure no one was around to see him, Minuti hopped out, propped the letter against the jug, then found a hiding place from which to wait and watch.

Sure enough, when Sun came into the room for a drink, he found the letter declaring Kimanuele's wish to marry his daughter. "Look at this, Moon!" roared Sun to his wife, brandishing the letter, sounding utterly amazed. "Such a bold one, this Kimanuele. How in the world did he manage to get a letter up here?" And with that he wadded up the paper and tossed it away. That night, when the maidens were readying themselves to return to earth for more water, Minuti the frog slipped unseen back into one of the clay jugs and was returned to earth. "Your letter has been delivered," Minuti told the chief. "But there was no reply. If I may suggest, you should have your son write yet another, and in six days I will try again."

And this he did, traveling to heaven the same way as

before, then hiding in the corner of Sun's chambers until he came in to drink. This time Sun wrote a reply, and by the following morning, Minuti was standing before the chief with it firmly in hand. "Surely you are among the cleverest of all men," it began. "I will grant your wish to marry my daughter, but first you must deliver to me her dowry—a heap of precious gold." And so Minuti was sent back to heaven two more times, each time carrying a bag of gold; Sun then wrote back, saying it was enough, that Kimanuele could come at his pleasure to claim his bride. "What now, good frog?" said Kimanuele sadly, fearing they'd reached the end of the road. "No matter how much I may wish it, I'll never be able to fly to the heavens."

But Minuti was not deterred, not even for a minute. That night he rose yet again into the heavens by way of a clay water jug and waited quietly until everyone had fallen fast asleep. Then he hopped into the daughter's bedroom and spread a thin layer of a strange liquid across her eyes. Sleeping in the corner of the room, he was jolted awake several hours later by the daughter's panicked cries. "Father, Mother, I am blind! I am blind! All the world is darkness!"

"It's a spell cast by her suitor," said the wise old doctor summoned to her bed. "Take her to earth, and he will surely cure her." So Sun set his spiders to spinning the most fantastic web, stretching all the way to earth—strong enough to hold his daughter and her attendants, yet so beautiful it would amaze anyone who chanced to gaze on it. By the next morning Minuti was back on earth reporting the developments to Kimanuele and his father, suggesting that they begin preparations for the wedding. Sure enough, five days later the daughter of Sun and Moon was lowered to earth, accompanied by the water maidens, who left her sitting by the secret pond. (By the way, as that beautiful web was being hauled back up to heaven, by chance it snagged on a handful of stars, creating that ribbon of light we call the Milky Way.) When the maidens were gone, Minuti hopped over and washed the young woman's eyes with the juice of a powerful purple berry, restoring her vision in time for her to see the soft light of dawn spreading across the earth. She sat there for a time transfixed, overwhelmed by the beauty of it all, listening as Minuti the wise frog told her the story of how this all came to be.

Of all the weddings that occurred in the centuries since, none has been more grand or celebrated. It's because of Minuti's nearly miraculous accomplishment, helping the son of a great chief marry the daughter of Sun and Moon, that to this day frogs are known as the wisest of all the creatures of Africa. ✹

# THE GIFT OF
# THE RAINBOW

(PHILIPPINES)

*The folklore of almost every culture is filled with fanciful
stories about rainbows. In Norse mythology, the rainbow was
a guarded bridge linking humans with the gods. The light
seen in the bands was caused by a fire burning on the bridge
that was intended to keep giants from crossing over. In other
times and places, rainbows have been the bow of the thunder
god or a giant snake coming out to feed on rivers and lakes,
later giving the water back to the earth in the form of rain.*

I T WAS AN especially fine day, and Bathala, source
of all graces, decided it was time to leave the heavens
and travel down to earth, time to bring happiness to
the people there. And so he set about summoning his
seven children to tell them of his planned journey and bid
them farewell. One by one they came to his side, his sons
Kidlat, the lightning; Araw, the sun; and Hangin, the wind;
and his daughters Liwayway, the dawn; Tag-ani, the goddess
of the harvest; and Tala, the star. But Bighani, the Goddess
of Flowers, never came. "Where is your sister?" Bathala
asked the other children, but they just stood there looking
sheepish, saying nothing. Finally, prodded by their father's
growing anger, one of the sisters confessed that Bighani was
again playing in the garden on earth, dancing with the plants,
compelling them to bloom.

"Very well," Bathala said, his voice full of thunder. "That is where she will stay. Alone and forevermore."

And so it was. That evening, try as she might, Bighani could not find her way out of the garden. Late at night a spirit finally came and told her of her father's decision, and she wept. Bighani lived for many years in that garden, and with each passing season it became more beautiful. Neighbors came often, drawn by her handiwork—colors and perfumes like none they'd ever encountered. One day someone suggested building a shrine to Bighani, a gift of thanks for all the beauty she'd brought into their lives. And so there was erected at the entrance to the garden a towering arch that could be seen from far away, covered with beautiful flowers.

As tends to happen with fathers, the time came when Bathala's anger with Bighani crumbled and blew away, leaving him with a tremendous longing for her company. One morning he summoned a spirit to go tell Bighani that it was time to come home. Yet for all her happiness at the thought of returning to her father's kingdom, Bighani knew she would miss the good people she'd come to know. As a keepsake she carried to heaven the bloom-covered bower that marked the entrance to the garden.

It's easy to tell when the Goddess of Flowers is on her way back to Earth's gardens. Hanging in the sky from her hands you can see that lovely bower, the arch of glowing colors we call rainbow. ✹

# QUEEN BERENICE'S HAIR

(GREECE)

*The following legend—which links the creation of the constellation Coma Berenices to the hair of a great queen—is hardly the only tale about this ethereal-looking group of stars. In the seventeenth century, an amateur astronomer using a homemade telescope saw a veil bearing a perfect likeness to Jesus in this constellation; this discovery, he claimed, was clearly linked to the Herodian princess said to have lent Christ her veil to wipe His brow on His final walk to the cross, only to later find the Savior's image miraculously impressed on the cloth.*

N SOME CLEAR, dark evening, cast your eyes to a slice of sky north of the constellation Virgo, where you'll find a small gathering of stars, faint and finely knit like a veil of lace, like the shimmering web of some great spider of the night. Or as people knew it long ago, the silken hair of Queen Berenice.

It was a perilous time in the kingdom. War had broken out with the Assyrians; messengers flocked to the palace every day, carrying news of death, like ravens. One morning the king announced that he would personally lead his soldiers into battle, and a fear spilled through Queen Berenice like none she'd ever known. The day her beloved rode off to war, the queen made a vow. Should he come home safely, to the goddess Aphrodite she would offer her most precious possession, her waist-length, amber hair, the most beautiful in all the kingdom.

Nor did she forget that promise when the king returned victorious. Taking a knife from the palace kitchen, she cut those lovely tresses, then carefully laid them in the temple of Aphrodite. Try to imagine the horror when she and the king arose the next day, and strolled out to the temple to find that the hair had been stolen! Berenice was shattered. The king blustered about, swearing vengeance against the scoundrel who would stoop so low as to steal a sacred gift from the queen.

And then late one night there was a knock on the door of the royal chambers. "Forgive me, Sire," the manservant said timidly. "But the court astronomer is asking for you. He implores you to come right away." And so the royal couple rose from their bed, rubbed the sleep from their eyes, and climbed the steep stairway leading up to the rooftop observatory, where Conon the astronomer was pacing excitedly.

"My King! My Queen! I have astonishing news." And he pointed to that faint gathering of stars just north of the constellation Virgo. "It was Jupiter who took your hair, my Queen. He has hung it in the night sky, where it will shine forevermore." ✸

# WHEN SUN
# MARRIED MOON

(TOGO, AFRICA)

*Many Africans believe in an ultimate God supported by minor spirits like Sun and Moon. Lesser deities commonly have human traits, while God himself is much harder to pin down. About God, however, it can at least be said that those on earth often have direct experiences of Him. People might describe a warm spell by saying "God is hot today," or during a winter shower, they might tell us that "God is falling as rain."*

HE KRACHI PEOPLE of Togo tell us that long ago, Sun and Moon decided to get married, and in the years that followed gave birth to all the stars in the sky. Unfortunately, in time the marriage began to sour, and one day Moon, restless creature that she is, decided to take a lover. When Sun found out about this, he was so furious he told his wife she was no longer welcome in the house. The two divided their possessions, and after much debate agreed that some of the children would go live with Moon, while the rest would remain with Sun.

Ever since this split, Moon sometimes gets restless and dissatisfied, at which point she gathers up her children and takes a trip back to her husband's fields. To say that the children of Sun and Moon don't get along during these outings is putting it mildly; in fact, it's the fierceness of their bickering that causes storms on earth. Fortunately, Moon has never been one to let such squabbles go on for long, and eventually she sends a messenger to pacify the children by waving a beautiful cloth of many colors—a cloth we call rainbow.

If Sun is in a particularly foul mood when he spots Moon in his fields, he may actually try to seize and eat her. We know this fit of anger as an eclipse. In times past when people saw this happening, they would come together to shout and beat their drums, thereby frightening Sun into letting Moon go free. ✸

# HARE STEALS THE SUN

(BANANZWA, SOUTHERN AFRICA)
*Many tales of the wily hare eventually found their way to*
*America via a West African slave known as Uncle Remus.*
*Today Hare still commands a great deal of respect from*
*people throughout Africa, some of whom claim he possesses*
*powers far beyond those of most other animals.*

INCE THE BEGINNING of time all creatures
have been blessed with certain gifts that help them
travel through this life. Some are strong and some
are fierce; some can run like the wind and some can
make beautiful music. But when it comes to the gift of cleverness, there is none to match the hare. Where others see
problems, he sees open doors; when most are giving up,
Hare is busy hatching some new crafty trick. Given that, it
should come as no surprise that much of what we think of as
commonplace on earth today can be traced back to the
doings of Hare.

One day Hare was out walking, stopping now and then to
lie in the grass and play his mbira (which, I must say, he
played as beautifully as anyone), when he came upon a spiderweb dangling from the heavens. Curious as to where it
might lead, he began climbing the strands until he found
himself in the most remarkable country, high up in the sky.
Being hungry after the long climb, he made his way to the
Chief's house and offered to play the mbira in exchange for

food. Well, the Chief had never heard anything so beautiful. Not only did he give Hare a feast of his best food, but he insisted that he stay the night, housed with the young girls of the village. The next morning Hare was amazed to see the girls open a huge pot sitting in the corner of the room, take out something they called the sun, and place it in the sky. When evening came they plucked the sun from the sky, stuck it back into the pot, and took out something called the moon. Hmmm, said Hare, thinking to himself (he was always thinking), what a grand thing it would be to have a sun on earth! So he waited until the girls went out to do their chores and sliced off a piece of the sun with his knife; then he ran as fast as his legs would carry him, back to the spiderweb and down to earth.

To say the Chief was angry about this bit of thievery is putting it mildly. With a party of his best warriors, he set off in pursuit of Hare, climbing down the web, then following his footprints across the countryside. Along the way they enlisted the help of the animals—leopards and lions, hyenas, birds, and baboons. As soon as he realized he was being pursued, Hare lined the trail with devil thorns in hopes of discouraging his pursuers. When that didn't work, he made a great rain fall so that his footprints would be washed away. But still they came. Finally, just as the group was almost upon him, he lay down beside the river, which was swollen in flood, and turned himself into a log. When the leader of the search party reached the bank, he was baffled. Where could he have gone? Suddenly one of the animals in the party thought he saw Hare hiding behind a rock on the other side of the river, so he picked up the log and threw it across the river to the other bank, trying to hit whatever it was sitting there. At the moment the log hit the ground, it turned back into Hare, who was of course now safe from his pursuers. He climbed to the highest branch of a tall tree, reached up into the sky, and hung the sun for all on earth to see.

Seeing the beauty of that sun, feeling its warmth, Baboon was heard to say that perhaps stealing was not always such a bad thing. "Now we can live in the light," he told the others. "Were it not for Hare, we'd still all be stumbling around in the dark." Ever since then, Baboon and all his relations, including humans, have shown an uncanny fondness for stealing things.

As for Hare, he lived on to spin other adventures in other times. But none was more amazing than the day he stole the sun. ✸

# THE MAIDEN RESCUED BY THE MOON

(SIBERIA)

*This story comes from the Tunguses, whose homeland is an enormous sprawl of land between the Yenisei River and the Pacific Ocean. They are a nomadic people, traveling without even tents, taking their shelter in caves and, occasionally, in the hollows of trees. Trees are important to these people for another reason as well: When the time is right, expectant mothers head to the forest to give birth, letting the woods be the place where infants are first welcomed into the world.*

LONE OLD WOMAN and her daughter made their camp on the lonely shore of the ocean. Each had a long list of chores that needed to be done each day, one of which was fetching washing and cooking water from the sea. Late one afternoon with the sun sinking low in the west, the mother looked around for water but the bucket was empty. "Daughter!" she called out, irritated. "Where is my water?" The daughter heard the tone in her voice and hurried back to camp, grabbed the wooden bucket and ladle, and trotted off down to the edge of the sea.

Now, this was a good girl, kind and well intentioned, but alas, she had a mind prone to wandering, and on this particular evening she was struck by the beauty of the last soft light dancing off the ocean waves. She stood there for the longest time, soaking up the sight, forgetting all about her chore. Finally her mother, unable to imagine what had become of her, walked out to the edge of camp and started scolding. "Has the water king taken you away, or what?" she cried, mentioning the girl by name.

One thing you must never do is call a girl standing in or near the water by name, for that is like delivering a written invitation to the water king to steal your loved one. And that is just what happened. Reaching up out of the sea, the water king wrapped his cold arms around the girl, who still held the ladle in her hand, and struggled to drag her under the waves. As it happened, the moon had just risen out of the water for its trek across the sky, and when it passed, the girl reached out with her free arm and caught hold of a bush growing on the moon's surface, then held on with all her might. Up she went, out of the chilling grasp of the water king, up into the heavens, where she has been ever since. If you look close, you will see her there, still holding on to that bush, the wooden ladle still in her hand. ✴

# CROW SAVES THE SUN

( JAPAN )
*Many cultures use nature myths to define the characteristics of various animals. And yet, taken as a whole they rarely condemn an animal absolutely. After all, animals—just like humans—have both positive and negative qualities. Surely we can forgive Crow of his bossy, boisterous ways when we learn of the great favor he did for humans at God's request.*

I N DAYS OF OLD, just like now, fierce battles often broke out between the gods of good and beings like the Black One, a fierce purveyor of darkness and destruction. The Black One, it seemed, never rested; he was always on the lookout for ways to foil the plans of the benevolent deities. One of his best chances to wreak havoc, or so he thought, came when humans finally began walking the earth. What is it, the Black One wondered to himself, that men and women cannot possibly live without? Suddenly it was clear to him. The sun! Without that they would perish in no time at all. And so he set about making plans to remove the sun from the sky the next morning—to swallow it, in fact, as it started its daily climb into the heavens.

Sure enough, the next day as the sun began to rise above the east horizon, the Black One was lying in wait, his big mouth open, ready to swallow it up. As chance would have it, though, the gods of kindness were well aware of the scheme, and created a special bird to foil it. That bird was the crow.

At the last second Crow appeared, seemingly out of nowhere, and flew right down the Black One's throat, making him choke, spoiling his evil plans.

Crow knows all too well that saving humankind from an icy death on a sunless earth is no small thing. He figures that humans should be beholden to him for such a courageous act—be perfectly willing, in fact, to let him feast on whatever food happens to be lying in the fields or growing in the gardens. And truthfully, who can argue? So the next time you think Crow altogether too bold, even a shameless thief, do try to remember that favor of long ago. ✸

# MOON IS HUNG
# IN THE SKY

(MANDINGO, AFRICA)

*Here's a wonderful example of how myths grow and change
to reflect new realities in the culture. As the use of iron
became a mainstay of the Mandingo culture, this beautiful
creation story came in its wake. Artwork surrounding this
story often shows the blacksmith climbing up to heaven not on
a rope—as would have been the case in earlier times—but on
an iron chain.*

HERE WAS A TIME on earth when there
was no such thing as death, nor was there any
moon hanging in the sky. People lived much as
they do now, raising families, working hard for
food and shelter, telling their stories. But when they grew
weary with work or were taken by sickness or old age, they
simply walked over to a long chain that hung down from the
clouds and climbed up to begin life anew in the heavens. Living in those days was a brawny, hard-working man by the
name of Fazog Bo Si, a blacksmith by trade, and father of
several daughters. Being a blacksmith was not easy work;
coal had to be hauled to the fire every day and heated using
hand bellows, and the iron had to be pounded and shaped
into tools. And Fazog Bo Si didn't have sons or apprentices
to lend a hand. It was only him, sweating sunup to sundown
beside the roaring fires of that forge.

Over the years his neighbors tried to cheer him, but they knew all too well that Fazog Bo Si was growing tired of his life. He talked less and less, and his head and broad shoulders began to slump, as if it had become an effort to move from chore to chore. It came as no surprise that one day, right in the middle of work, Fazog Bo Si simply walked away from his forge, not even bothering to put down the big chunk of iron he'd been heating; he headed over to the chain that hung down from the clouds and lifted himself off the ground and into the heavens. As it happened, his daughters were nearby and saw all this, and the eldest told the others that they should follow. "And another thing," she said. "Once we reach the sky, we'll pull up the chain so that no one will be able to follow." And that is exactly what they did. It was when that chain was hoisted up, that precious link to heaven pulled out of reach, that men and women on earth began to know of death.

As for that piece of iron the blacksmith had in his big right hand, still hot from the forge, that became the moon. Even today when the crescent moon rises in the west, people will point to it and say that Fazog Bo Si is starting to heat his chunk of iron; naturally, the metal glows bigger and brighter the longer it's in the forge, and so several days later, when it's fully heated, those of us on earth see that as a full moon. The blacksmith's daughters are up there in the sky, too; on clear nights you can look up and see them as a cluster of stars, huddled around their beloved father. ✸

# RAIN COMES
# TO EARTH

(WEST AFRICA)

*Liberia is connected to many other countries in West Africa—*
*especially Guinea, Sierra Leone, and the Ivory Coast—*
*through an intriguing web of related myths. In some cases,*
*the only real difference among stories from these countries*
*is that there are different characters in the starring roles.*
*Elephant may play the lead role in a land where there are*
*many elephants, while Goat will play that same role in*
*places where goats are common.*

E BEGIN IN THE DAYS when Meleka lived in a small, isolated corner of the heavens, high above the rings of clouds that sometimes cradle the world. In case you didn't know, Meleka is considered the greatest of the gods, having made the world and all that's in it—birds and bats and people, rocks and rivers and trees. Meleka and his wife had a beautiful little girl named Sia, which means "first-born." How loved that child was! Sia was a sensitive child, prone to crying at the drop of a hat, never more so than when she looked down from the clouds and saw the hurtful ways of humans. Whenever that happened, Meleka himself became enraged with the men and women who made his daughter unhappy, and as often as not would take out his sword and thrash about, causing the most extraordinary peals of lightning and thunder. This upset Sia more, and she wept even harder, her tears falling as great torrents of rain to the earth below. Now, because Meleka and his family lived in just one place, having a daughter who cried so much meant that part of the world directly below grew soggy, then flooded, and finally turned into a great ocean.

The consequences of this were hardly lost on Meleka. He could see that one part of the world was becoming water-logged, while the rest of it remained dry. He thought and thought about what to do, then summoned the winds. "The solution is simple," he told them. "You must blow my family about—to and fro, here and there," which the winds were only too happy to do. Thus during the years that followed, rain spread well beyond that one ocean, turning the hills green near and far, making lush forests and fields, watering flowers and crops. As the years passed, Meleka became ever more grateful to the winds, not just because they'd done what he had commanded, but because they carried his daughter about on their backs as if she was the most precious cargo in all the heavens. Which of course she was.

Throughout West Africa there are those yet today called on to summon rain in times of drought. One of the first things these shamans do is speak with those who know Sia best: the winds. They ask the winds and the clouds her whereabouts and offer through them invitations that Sia might come again, that she might bring her tears to thirsty lands. ✹

# HOW BROKEN LOVE MADE THE MOON AND NORTH STAR

(NIGERIA)

*One of the most enchanting aspects of many African folk-tales is the notion that there was a time when heaven hung close to the earth and was accessible to humans by ropes hanging down from the sky.*

NE SPECIAL CUSTOM surrounded marriage even in the old days, when neither moon nor stars hung in the night sky, and every couple, rich or poor, was bound to it like skin to the fruit. The families of young women about to wed cooked a traditional pot of walnuts, then shared them the next day with their prospective in-laws. If the walnuts were prepared properly—and they almost always were—this boded well for the couple, suggesting that they would remain happy for many years. But if the walnuts came out badly, it was a sure sign that the marriage was doomed to not work out. No prospective bride or her family took this custom lightly; great care went into finding the very best walnuts, and they were tended through the night with the utmost care.

On the night before the feast for beautiful Imola, around midnight a cold rain began, unlike any storm the villagers had seen in years. Now, while this rain didn't have any direct effect on the cooking of the walnuts, the family members who'd been tending the pot ended up running inside to their sleeping mats to escape the downpour, leaving the pot unwatched until dawn. It was then that a certain wicked woman, the second wife of Imola's father, crept up to the cooking fire and threw armload after armload of wood onto the embers, creating flames so hot they soon burned the walnuts to a crisp.

At the time there was no such thing as suicide. But if ever there was grief sharp enough to move someone to end her life, it was rooted in Imola's heart. When no one was looking, Imola crept out behind the house and began praying. "God, if you are truly my creator, then drop down a rope from the sky. I want no more of this life." And in a short time a rope did indeed drop from the clouds, the loose end coming to rest in front of Imola's tear-stained face. It wasn't until she was halfway to heaven that someone happened to look up and see what was going on. Shouts went up and Imola's family came running, her father and mother calling frantically, pleading with her to come back. But this was the end of Imola's life on earth. As she reached the bottom of the clouds, it was almost dark; it was then that her body began to glow white, changing into the moon we see today.

Imola's family hadn't been the only ones pleading with her that day to return; her lover had also tried to call her back to earth. The next evening, realizing that Imola was gone for good, he, too, called on God to send down a rope so that he might follow, and God did. Just before the young man reached the sky, he changed into the North Star; you can still see him up there, a star chasing his love, the moon, praying that one day they will be rejoined and marry still. ✹

*The*

# MAKINGS

*of*

# EARTH

# THE MAKING OF
# MOUNT SHASTA

(MODOC INDIANS, CALIFORNIA)
*It's difficult to imagine a mountain with the beauty and
stature of Shasta not being wrapped in legend and lore.
The Klamath Indians, a tribe located in Oregon, near the
Modocs, also have a tale about Mt. Shasta. They tell how
long ago the chiefs of the above and below worlds were locked
in a great battle—the leader of the above world taking posi-
tion on Shasta, and the ruler of the below world settling a
hundred miles to the north on Mount Mazama. The feud
ended when Mount Mazama collapsed, sending Llao, chief
of the below world, back underground. (Over time, water
collected in the hollow of this collapsed volcano, creating
Crater Lake.) It's interesting to note that the Klamath Indians
were living in the Mount Mazama area at the time of its
collapse. Did Shasta erupt around the same period, causing
the Klamaths to link two distant mountains together in a
single myth?*

IN THE FAR NORTH of California is a land where
the air runs thick with the smell of pine, where robes
of pussytoes and paintbrush and shooting stars fall
easy across the shoulders of the highlands. It's here
you'll find one of the great peaks of the West, a snow-
capped, cone-shaped mountain called Shasta, a volcanic
bridge between the worlds of earth and sky.

Now, it happened long ago that the Sky Spirit found the land above the clouds too cold for his liking, so taking his great stone drill in hand, he set about the enormous task of cutting a hole in the sky. When at last he finished, he gathered huge masses of snow and ice from the far reaches of the heavens and pushed them out through the freshly cut hole, where they fell to earth. Day after day he worked, until at last there was an icy mound rising thousands of feet in the air—a stepping stool for the Sky Spirit to climb down onto the barren skin of earth. Once on land, he created those things we see in the world today: the animals and birds, the trees and rivers, the grass and the flowers. Satisfied with his handiwork, he then climbed back into the sky, gathered his wife and children, and guided them back to a new home he'd made for them in the heart of the mountain. Many were the days you could have seen smoke from their lodge fires rising in great clouds from the top of Shasta; sometimes, when it was very cold, the family would throw enormous logs on the fire, building it so high that the earth would rumble with the burn.

As grand a life as it was on Earth, in time the Sky Spirit began to miss his old home in the heavens. One fine morning he quenched the fire inside the mountain, guided his family back up the flanks of Shasta, and disappeared again into the clouds.

# THE WHITE CLIFFS
# OF DOVER

(NETHERLANDS)

*The giants are at it again in this tale about how the Cliffs of Dover turned white. Not nearly so fanciful is the scientific explanation, which is that the cliffs are white because they're made of chalk.*

ANY ARE THE TALES from days when giants roamed the earth. There was the time, for example, when seven titans were hired to build the canal we know today as the Rhine River; upon finishing their work, each one knocked the dirt from his shovel, creating the seven Siebengebirge Hills near Bonn, Germany. And then there was that steely Hag of the Ridges, who made Scotland by dropping rocks and peat into the sea—a woman who liked to wash her clothes in the Corryvreckan whirlpools, then spread them to dry across the flanks of Mount Storr. And so, too, was it at the hands of giants that the White Cliffs of Dover came to be.

They were a crew of Goliaths, sailing their enormous ship from the cold roil of the North Sea into uncharted waters. On coming to the English Channel, the captain, who was not well seasoned, studied the passage for a time and concluded that his ship would indeed fit. But he was wrong. The hull creaked and groaned against the earth and finally stuck fast, the starboard side resting against a set of high cliffs. The captain was beside himself! He fussed and fretted and stomped about the deck, his feet sending shudders like claps of thunder through the sea. As it happened, one of the hands—just a boy, really—had an interesting idea; mustering all his courage, he went up and offered it to the snarling captain. "Beg pardon, Cap'n. But the grip isn't as tight as it might be. How about I take some of the men and we rub this hull with a good layer of soap?"

So that's what they did: gathered up every bar of soap on that ship and soaped the hull from top to bottom. And sure enough, pushed southward by the hand of a good gale, the colossal ship made it through. Of course, with a tight squeeze like that, most of the soap was scraped off onto the cliffs, which is what turned them white. What's more, if you've ever stood and watched the sea break against the toes of that precipice, you've probably noticed those waves are chock full of foam. Now you know why.

# THE COMING OF WATER

(KWAKIUTL INDIANS, BRITISH COLUMBIA)
*Many generations of Kwakiutl Indian have spent winter nights huddled around longhouse fires, sharing stories from the beautiful braid of forest, river, and ocean that marks their homelands in western British Columbia.*

IN THE SEASON of the long ago, the world was a parched place, dry as old bones. Every day people and animals alike struggled to quench their thirst; some gathered the dew off blades of grass, while others held their tongues against the roots of plants in the chance of gaining a few drops of moisture. There was an old woman in those days living near what is now Bull Harbor, and on a table in her kitchen was a rock bowl filled to the brim with water she'd collected from the dripping roots around her house. One morning Raven, who was always well informed about such matters, headed over to the old woman's house, a stick of wood in his hand. "Please forgive the bother," he told the woman, "but I have no cooking fire. Might I collect some of yours on this stick to fix my breakfast?" The woman nodded without a word, and motioned him inside.

Raven was bent over the fireplace, stirring the coals, when he spotted the rock bowl full of water on the kitchen table. "I hesitate to ask," he said to the woman, "but my throat is so dry. Could I have a small drink of your water?"

"I suppose," the woman said, frowning. "But take only a sip."

As soon as Raven's beak hit the water, he started guzzling it like there was no tomorrow. This upset the woman terribly, and she ran over and shooed him away, yelling about how it was her water, after all, not his. Back at the fireplace again, poking in the coals with his stick, as soon as the woman wasn't looking, Raven bent down and rolled his tongue in some of the ashes at the edge of the fire. "Look," he told the woman, opening his mouth. "I'm still dry as can be. Perhaps just one more swallow?" The woman was reluctant, but in the end she agreed.

When she looked over from her cook pot, though, there was Raven gulping away, draining the very last drops! The woman grabbed the stick Raven had left by the fireplace and ran across the room with it held high, planning to whack him over the head. But Raven, being quick, jumped off the table just as the stick fell, then flew out the door like a blast of wind. He climbed high into the sky and headed for home, and as he made his way, drops of water fell from his beak. Where each drop fell, streams and lakes appeared—even rivers, like the beautiful Fraser and the mighty Columbia.

And that's how water came to a dry land.

# GIANT LEVELS A MOUNTAIN

(JAVA, INDONESIA)
*This tale is one of two told in Java about women trying to avoid a bad marriage by assigning their suitors impossible tasks. In the other story, a banished queen is horrified to discover that the man she has fallen in love with and is about to marry is her own son. Unwilling to break the news, she tells him the day before the wedding that he must prove his love by building not only a beautiful boat on which to hold a celebration feast but also a lake to sail it on—all in a single night! Much to the queen's horror, the man succeeds. The queen prays to Brahma to intervene, which he does by breaking loose the earthen dam that holds the lake in place. The son is lost to the rushing water emptying out of the lake, and the grief-stricken mother throws herself into the water and drowns. Geologists have confirmed that while the place where all of this supposedly happened is a marshy plain today, back in the Stone Age the basin did in fact hold a massive lake.*

CONSIDER NOW THIS TALE of fear and cleverness, spun thousands of years ago, when giants still roamed the earth at will. One day while out sitting in the garden with her father the king, a certain princess looked up to see a sour-looking giant crashing through the forest in the distance, making his way for the palace grounds. She was alarmed, naturally, but her father told her to remain still, that it was no use running from the brute, for there was no door he could not open, no wall he could not topple with the mere nudge of his massive elbows.

In a matter of minutes the giant was standing before them, his big bare feet planted squarely in a bed of orchids, his hair as wild and unkempt as a patch of beach grass. "King," he bellowed, "for months I've been eyeing this beautiful daughter of yours. It's my wish to marry her, and I've come to ask your permission to do just that." At which point the princess felt her throat swell and her head begin to throb. The king, sensing her alarm, reached over and calmly laid his hand on her shoulder, but in truth, his own stomach was churning at the thought of such a thing, his head buzzing as he struggled for the right way to respond. One did not, after all, insult a giant without risking terrible consequences. Finally the king spoke, sounding far more sure of himself than he really was. "You may marry my daughter," he said, "but there is one condition. You must level Tengger Mountain in a single night." Now, to the giant this actually seemed reasonable. No one would be allowed to marry the king's daughter, after all, without some proof of wealth or character. "That's fair," he told the king, and without another word he stomped out of the garden, plucked a giant coconut shell from the ground to use as a scoop, and went after that mountain with abandon. Around midnight the king and his daughter went out to check on the giant's progress and, much to their horror, found he was very far along with the task, to the point where it seemed he might actually succeed!

That's when the princess had an idea. Around three

o'clock, still well before dawn, she went over to the hen house and poked at the rooster, waking him up. Annoyed at the intrusion, the rooster began crowing like crazy; when the giant heard this, he concluded that morning must be just minutes away. Looking down and realizing he had at least another hour or two of work, he shook his head, dropped the coconut shell in a huff, and walked off, never to return to that part of the country again. The crater he left behind we know today as Tengger caldera. As for that giant coconut shell he used for a shovel, it's still there, too, overturned beside Mount Bromo, covered by a steep, rutted pile of cinders.

# THE HILLS OF
# ACHIK ASONG

(INDIA)
*This story of how a range of hills known as Jajong Kadoram
came to be is a favorite among the peasant dwellers of Asam.*

LONG AGO, in that beautiful land known as
Achik Asong, there lived an honest, generous man
named Jarang. You would have needed to share
only a few minutes with Jarang to know that he
considered his greatest blessings to be his wife and son; in
fact, those who knew him best said he loved them too much,
that in wanting to give them everything, he'd indulged them
until both were spoiled beyond reason.

One evening Jarang was sitting in the courtyard with his
beloved family when the full moon topped the horizon,
bathing them in the finest silky light, causing everyone to
catch their breath. Far from being satisfied, though, Jarang's
son ran over to his father and insisted that he fetch this fine
moon for him to play with. With great patience Jarang
kneeled down next to his son and explained that not only did
the moon live far away, but that there wasn't even a road by
which to reach it. But his son would hear none of it. First he
threw a tantrum that lasted for days. Then he refused to eat,
becoming run down and hollow cheeked. Jarang's wife was
incensed—not at her son, mind you, but at her husband,
chastising him for not even making an honest attempt to grab

the moon. "All you have to do is build a stairway," she scolded him. Fearing his wife's scowls and his son's ill health even more than the ordeal of such a task, Jarang finally gave in. He paid a visit to his nephew, and the two of them set off to build a stairway into the heavens and fetch the moon.

After many months their staircase towered high above the earth, nearly to the clouds. Even Jarang was pleased. One day, running low on bamboo, he yelled down instructions from the top stair tread to his nephew on the ground below. What he said was "I need more bamboo! I need more bamboo!" What his nephew heard, however, was "I've got the moon! I've got the moon!" This was a most unfortunate misunderstanding, since at the point Jarang had the moon secured, his nephew was to chop down the staircase, leaving Jarang to float back to earth with the moon in his arms. As per that plan, sure enough the nephew took the ax and chopped down the pillars of the staircase, with Jarang's wife and son looking on. Of course, poor Jarang fell like a rock from the sky. His wife and son waited and waited for him to show up at the house, day after day, then began searching for him. When they couldn't locate him, both grew angry, certain that Jarang had simply abandoned them, and was now living the good life somewhere in the sky.

Though Jarang's body never was found, when that mammoth staircase toppled to earth, it did so with a mighty crash, creating a choppy line of hills known as Jajon Kadoram, which can still be seen today in Achik Asong. You can walk their crests, formed by those ancient heaps of bamboo, and wonder at a man who loved his family so much that he would try to give them the moon.

# GLACIER OF TEARS

(NEW ZEALAND)
*The race of Polynesians known as the Maori are especially fond of storytelling. They not only relish tales of creation like this one, but are also dedicated to creating new legends out of major events in modern times.*

ANY ARE THE TRAVELERS who come to the South Island of New Zealand and stand open-mouthed at the foot of the beautiful Franz Joseph Glacier, named for the former Emperor of Austria. Yet the native Maori call this grand massif of ice by a far more poetic name: the Tears of the Avalanche Girl.

A long time ago there lived a fine young man and great hunter of the plains by the name of Wawe. As fate would have it, Wawe had betrothed to him a beautiful young woman from the high country of the South Island named Hine-hukatere. Here was truly a woman of the mountains, a person whose heart seemed to open fully only when she was out roaming the icy summits and snow fields of the highlands. As you might imagine, this cold, abrupt land was quite strange to Wawe. But he cared deeply for Hine, and after they wed, hardly a week went by when he didn't suggest they climb the heights together on some long, wild outing to her beloved mountains.

Being from the plains, Wawe was not nearly so sure of foot

as Hine in that jumble of rock and ice and crevice. One day while the couple was crossing a steep slope, poor Wawe's feet slipped right out from under him; the last sound Hine heard was a mournful cry as he plummeted over a sheer cliff, meeting his death on the rocks below. Hine was so overcome with grief, so full of regret that her love for these windswept mountains had in a way contributed to the death of her husband, that she couldn't bring herself to move another step. She lay down on the snow and began crying. Day after day her tears flowed, running across the snow and down the cliff into the valley below. When the gods of winter looked down and saw what was happening, they were greatly saddened. In the end they decided to turn those tears into a river of ice— what we call Franz Joseph Glacier—a monument to the heartbreak of that maiden of the high mountains.

# WHY THERE ARE EARTHQUAKES

(KOREA)

*Many folktales tell of heaven departing from its original place near the surface of the earth because of a human offense. This story has a much different and fairly unusual twist, telling of a Herculean effort to keep heaven from crashing down from its lofty place in the sky.*

I T MAY SURPRISE YOU to learn that long ago, back at the beginning of time, even heaven had its share of problems. But of all those troubles, none alarmed the king more than the day he woke to find that one of the corners of paradise had begun to sag. He summoned his servants, startling them with the worry in his voice. "Heaven is sagging," the king told them. "Either we stop it, or one day—not long from now—it will topple and crash to the ground." And with that he dispatched his most trusted workers to earth to build an enormous pillar of red copper and place it under heaven's sagging floor. Unfortunately, the ground where the pillar rested gave way under all the weight, and before long the kingdom was just as bad off as before.

What to do? Many came forward with ideas for how to solve the problem—some good, some rather silly—but nothing seemed to work. Finally the king set off through the streets of heaven, determined to find the strongest man in all the kingdom. And what a strong man he found! "Heaven is collapsing," he told the man, and went on to describe the problem in great detail. "I want you to go down to Earth, spread your feet wide apart, and heft that copper pillar onto your shoulder." The strong man did just that, and has been doing so ever since.

As you might imagine, after a while all that weight can make even a strong man's shoulder tired and sore. When that happens, the man carefully shifts the pillar to his other shoulder, a move that takes so much effort that the very earth beneath his feet shakes with the trembling in his legs. So the next time you feel a quivering in the earth—what we call an earthquake—know that it is simply the strong man struggling to reposition the pillar of heaven.

# THE BEACHES OF TARANAKI

(NEW ZEALAND)

*Even today there seems a certain magic to the beautiful*
*Taranaki Province, which takes its name from a giant who*
*once fought a fierce battle for the love of a beautiful woman*
*giant living nearby named Tongariro. Badly burned by his*
*rival, he was forced down to the edge of the sea to soak his*
*wounds, where he has remained ever since, standing as a*
*great mountain, his profile not unlike the glorious Mount*
*Fuji of Japan. Winds from the Tasman Sea regularly blow*
*up and over Taranaki (now called Mount Egmont), where*
*they chill and fall as rain on the province, creating mile after*
*mile of rich, green pastures—the heart of the New Zealand*
*dairy lands.*

B ACK WHEN New Zealand was very young, long
before the coming of the *pakeha* (white people),
the descendants of Turi lived blessed lives on
Taranaki. It was a good land, overflowing with
birds and plants and fish, bountiful in ways that spurred generosity of spirit in all who made their homes there. One
spring morning after a great storm at sea, two canoes washed
up on the rocks of the Taranaki coast. Sitting in one, looking
frightened and exhausted, were two young women from
Hawaiki who had been traveling to see relatives, while the
other canoe was filled with gifts and clothes and other per-

sonal possessions. It was obvious from the way these young women spoke and dressed that they were of high social rank. And that is just how the people of Taranaki treated them, feeding and tending them with great respect and kindness, repairing the damage done to their canoes, reprovisioning them so they could resume their trip when it pleased them to do so.

When the young women returned home, their father, a noble chief, was greatly relieved, for he had thought them surely lost at sea. On hearing how generous the residents of Taranaki had been, he knew right away that he must find a way to thank those kindly strangers. "Is there anything they need?" he asked his daughters. The women thought long and hard, but it seemed those people had everything anyone could ever want. Then one of the daughters had an idea. "There is one thing lacking," she told her father. "On their beaches all you will find is rocks and cobbles and boulders— hard things that hurt the feet and damage the bottoms of canoes."

"That's it!" said their father, obviously relieved. And with that he called out to the people of the village to fill his largest canoe with the soft, black sand that lay along the coastline. This was the gift he sent to Taranaki, scattering it along the shores, covering the rocks and the cobbles, piling it into a vast braid of dunes and sandpiles that the people enjoy to this day.

# CASCADE MOUNTAINS BLOCK THE RAIN

(NATIVE AMERICANS, PACIFIC NORTHWEST)

*In most cultures, including those of many Native Americans, the building of mountains or other prominent land features is often attributed to giants. In this case, however, the Creator himself reaches down from the sky to form the Cascades, as part of a punishment for people who have been greedy. This punishment may suggest just how serious an offense greed was thought to be.*

HEN THE WORLD was young there were no great mountains scraping the sky east of Puget Sound. The land rolled east from the ocean for hundreds of miles in a great yawn of grass and occasional pockets of trees, wide open and full of wind. In those days there was no such thing as rain; whatever water was needed by the people and plants and animals rose cool and pure from the unbroken ground. One fateful year, though, the water in what is now eastern Washington stopped coming, and all the living things began to thirst. Finally the situation got so bad that a delegation of leaders was sent west to plead for help from Ocean. Ocean was more than generous, calling on his own children, Clouds and Rain, to return with those desperate people and freshen the land.

Yet even after the land was again green and full of life, the people were not satisfied. For months they dug pit after pit and then insisted that Clouds and Rain fill them, even though Clouds and Rain had long since grown weary and wanted to go home. When Ocean heard what was happening, he sent word to the people that they needn't worry, they could count on him to send water on a regular basis, but they would not believe, choosing instead to dig more and more holes and force Ocean's children to fill them with rain. Finally Ocean's patience gave out, and he sent a fervent prayer to the Great Spirit that he might punish those people for their greedy ways.

And that is just what the Great Spirit did. One day He leaned down from the sky and with His massive hands scooped out enormous heaps of Earth from a place near the ocean, which would later fill with seawater and become Puget Sound. These loads of Earth He heaped higher and higher until He had fashioned the mighty Cascade Mountains. Ever since then these great peaks have been a wall that catches rain-laden clouds as they head inland and forces them up into the cold air where they chill and let loose their moisture, leaving precious little for lands lying farther to the east. Much of the water we find east of those great mountains is that which lies cool and still in the pits dug by the people of long ago: Palmer, Omak, and Spectacle lakes, and of course the biggest excavation of them all, fifty-five-mile-long Lake Chelan.

*The*

# NATURE

*of*

# THINGS

# CHILDREN LEARN TO WALK

(OJIBWA INDIANS, NORTH-CENTRAL
UNITED STATES AND CANADA)

*The wise hero of this story is Nanabush, one of four sons of
the West Wind. Each of these sons was charged with bring-
ing special gifts to the Ojibwa people—courage, romance, a
sense of beauty, and for Nanabush, humor and storytelling.*

I T WAS A LONG TIME AGO in the land of trees,
and Spirit Woman had given birth to human twins.
Every animal was fond of these twins, forever doting
on them, each eager to do whatever was needed to
make them warm and safe and happy. Dog, for one, never
left their side. Sometimes flies would come and pester the
children, and Dog would snap at them to make them fly
away. To amuse the children, he nuzzled their soft bellies
with his nose or jumped into the air and did all manner of
wonderful tricks. When the twins were hungry, Wolf and
Deer lent their milk, while Bear warmed them with his marvelous coat of fur. The birds sang them to sleep at night, and
Beaver washed them in the lake.

But over time it began to dawn on the animals that something was not quite right. "We feed them and care for them
like our own," said Bear, "yet they do not stand. They do not
run and play in the woods like our children do. Nanabush
will come soon. We must ask his help." A few days later,

when Nanabush, son of West Wind, arrived, the animals told him their concerns. Nanabush told the animals they had cared for the babies well. Too well. "Children grow by reaching, striving for what they want," he said. "Not by having everything placed in their laps. I will go and ask Great Spirit what to do."

So Nanabush left the woods and went high into the hills to the west, seeking the help of Great Spirit. When Great Spirit heard the problem, he told Nanabush to scour the slopes of those high hills for a certain kind of sparkling stone. "Gather as many as you can," he instructed, "and place them in a pile on the highest hill." Nanabush did just that, until he had an enormous pile of the colored stones, many times higher than a man's head. But what was he supposed to do next? Hour after hour he sat there, hoping for some further instruction from Great Spirit, but no word came. Finally out of boredom Nanabush began tossing the stones into the air, first one at a time, then big handfuls. Once he tossed several high into the air and they did not come back down again! Instead they changed into the most beautiful winged creatures—the very first butterflies.

When Nanabush returned to the children in the forest, he was surrounded by a flashing, fluttering blanket of butterflies. The twins were delighted, and set about waving and stretching to catch one in their chubby hands. For a long time they crawled after them, then stood on their tiny feet and tottered, and finally ran through the forest laughing, all the while hoping to catch even one of those beautiful flying creatures.

And that is how butterflies taught children to walk. 🦋

# THE COMING OF DARKNESS

(SIERRA LEONE, AFRICA)
*Across much of Africa people celebrate light coming to the world at each rising sun. Because of Africa's year-round warmth, however, there are few ceremonies to welcome back the sun at winter solstice—strikingly different from cultures in colder places like North America and Europe.*

HEN THE EARTH was very young, say the Kono people, there was no such thing as darkness. By day the sun would shine, slowly giving way to a moon that cast a beautiful, brilliant twilight throughout the night. One day God summoned Bat and instructed him to carry a special basket into the sky and give it to Moon. In the basket, God explained, was darkness, and though it came with no instructions, He assured Moon that one day soon He would be by to explain how it was to be used. So Bat lashed the basket to his back and off he flew.

Now, as you might imagine, such a long journey left Bat tired and hungry, and at one point along the way he stopped, set the basket down, and went off in search of food. In his absence a group of animals happened to stumble across this strange parcel and, thinking that it might contain something good to eat, decided to have a closer look. Bat returned just as they were prying off the lid, but by then it was too late. Darkness had escaped.

Ever since then Bat has slept all day long. Then each evening he rises from his slumber and begins flying frantically about, trying his best to gather the darkness, put it back into the basket, and take it to Moon as God commanded. Of course, his heroic efforts never really succeed, and by first light he is exhausted and must return to earth to sleep again. ☽

# THE STORY OF
# THE TIDES

(PHILIPPINES)

*Only recently has romantic love, rather than honor of duty or generosity, become one of the key driving forces in many of the world's nature stories. Among such tales, none portrays the anguish of unrealized romantic love better than "The Story of the Tides."*

 ONG AGO THE WORLD was woven into three separate kingdoms: Earth, Sea, and Sky. Each was ruled by a powerful god, all bound by a supreme law prohibiting them from ever entering into the affairs of the others. But this is a tale of love, and where love is concerned, even supreme laws can't always be abided.

The radiant daughter of the sky was Moon. She was a child filled with wanderlust, never missing an opportunity to explore the far reaches of the heavens. One morning in late spring she steered her chariot onto a dark, winding path she'd never seen before, at the end of which lay something stranger and more thrilling than anything she'd seen. It was the sea. Moon stood for hours on the shore, enchanted, overwhelmed by the sounds and smells and colors, the soothing roll of the waves.

"And who are you, beautiful one?" said a voice from behind, startling her. She turned to find a handsome, smiling young man, son of the great God of the Sea. A fondness took hold as the two of them talked through the afternoon, and more meetings came in the months that followed—once a week or so at first, then every few days, until finally not a day would pass when Moon did not journey to meet her new love at the edge of the sea.

One day Moon's cousin was visiting, and being the nosy sort, she decided to follow Moon down to the shore. On witnessing the romance, a great jealousy rose inside her, and she rushed back to the heavens to inform Moon's father, God of the Sky. The news that his daughter was willingly breaking one of the supreme laws made the sky god furious; when Moon returned, she found him waiting with burning eyes. "No more will you wander," he told her. "From this moment on you'll spend your days alone, here in the gardens of Heaven. And Moon," he added sternly, "know that I'll be posting guards, day and night, should you be tempted to stray."

With that he summoned a messenger to carry a note to the God of the Sea, telling him what had happened between their two children. And that god, too, seethed with anger—so much so, in fact, that he imprisoned his son in one of the great caves at the edge of the sea.

Now, being a clever goddess, Moon quickly discovered a way around the guards her father had posted, and rushed back to the shore. "Where are you?" she whispered over and over again to her lover. It was only by chance that he happened to look up from his prison cave that day and see her reflection in the water above. He charged the cave entrance, trying mightily to get out, rousing the entire sea. Day after day it went on—Moon hurrying down to the shore in her chariot, the handsome son of the sea god fighting to escape and rejoin her. Even now, when the people see the great swell of a high tide along the coast at full moon, they will say, "Look there. The son of the sea struggles to get out. He rushes to meet Moon."

# NORTHERN LIGHTS

(SWEDEN)

*Though the aurora borealis has probably been dancing across the heavens for some fifty million years, its location in the far north means that many fewer people have witnessed it than other heavenly curiosities, like rainbows and lightning and shooting stars. Yet the northern lights have never failed to fire the imaginations of those lucky enough to see them. Some cultures maintained that they were caused by an erupting volcano; others said it was simply the Laplanders, going about the mountains with torches, looking for lost reindeer.*

I N THE DISTANT PAST, when all the birds and animals still felt free to talk, it wasn't uncommon to hear them issuing challenges to one another, setting up contests to see who was strongest, or fastest, or even the most clever. And so it was one spring day in the reeds of a great southern lake, when two flocks of swans sat wrangling over which would likely be the first to reach summer range in Scandinavia. "There is only one way to find out," said the leader of the larger flock. "The race begins at first light."

Naturally, everyone was up early that day, stretching her wings, chortling to her opponents about how easy the trip would be for her and her flock of able flyers. As soon as the sun topped the east horizon, there was a great sweep of white wings as hundreds of birds left the lake, spiraling quickly into the sky, heading north. I'd like to say it was a close race, but it wasn't. The larger flock simply had stronger birds, and by the end of the first day, they had left their challengers far behind. By the time they finally settled on a perfect patch of summer ground in Scandinavia, the other flock was hours behind them, struggling on, clearly aware that they'd lost the great race.

It was pride, I suppose, that made them sweep high above the winning group of birds without the slightest whisper, continuing farther and farther to the north, never bothering to land in Scandinavia at all. By late the next day the birds were wearied to the bone, but more important, were nearing the farthest, most bone-chilling reaches of the world. At some point during that night the air became so bitter cold that the beautiful swans froze fast in the skies.

And that's where they've been ever since. Now and then some of them will, with great effort, manage to stir and rustle about slightly, and it's light reflecting off those fluttering white wings that makes the aurora borealis—what many of us like to call the northern lights. ♪

# FAIRY'S PIN WELL

(YORKSHIRE, ENGLAND)
*Besides gifts of coins, rags, buttons, flowers, and stones,*
*people have been tossing pins into the wells of Great Britain*
*since Roman times. Some claimed that if the pin discolored in*
*the water, it was a sign that the presiding deity of the well—*
*often a fairy—was pleased, and the person's wish would be*
*granted. Such offerings were more than popular; as late as the*
*1800s, the Ffynnon Fair Penrhys well in Wales was half full*
*of pins!*

S HE WAS A FINE ONE, this young Joan from
Selby—hard-working, kind to neighbors, and generous to strangers. It was hardly surprising when
she began to catch the attention of bachelors far
and wide. While it was nothing to pass on some of those
men, there was a handful of suitors, honest and forthright,
that in the end simply left her feeling terribly confused. It
was in that state of mind that one day she made a trek to the
top of the Hill of Brayton, high above the valley of Ouse, to
a small, spring-fed pool of water said to have powers for
young women in matters of love. As was the custom, while
climbing up the wooded knoll she thought all the while of
those few good men. On reaching the top, she drank of the
springwater and made her request to the well spirit. "Good
spirit of the well, bring to my dreams an image of him des-
tined to be my husband." With that she laid down and slept,

and sure enough, her head was soon filled with images of a fine young man—Robin the Bowyer.

Now, the Hill of Brayton, like most such pleasant places, was home to a tribe of woodland fairies. They knew Joan (fairies take special notice of mortals with good character), and on finding her asleep at the pool devised the most remarkable plan—something that would help them as well as all the young women of Selby. At the time these fairies were hunters, shooting their quarry with tiny vine bows and arrows made of thorns. It was the thorn arrows that proved to be the problem; they broke easily, and were almost impossible to shoot straight. As it happened, a month or so prior to Joan's visit another young woman had come to the spring to drink and ask for dreams of her future lover, and in doing so had lost a pin from her dress. The value of it as an arrow was obvious to the fairies.

As Joan slept, the fairies doused her eyelids with a magic dust that causes humans to wake in fairyland. And what an awakening it was. The moon was like something she'd never seen—a bright wash of silver light, charming, making her want to dance and sing from the sheer beauty of it. Even stranger was that everything seemed so incredibly big: The Hill of Brayton looked like a mountain, the spring pool a sprawling lake. And then, of course, the fairies themselves—dozens of them, gentlemen in suits of plaited grass, ladies in spiderweb dresses with colored embroidery, wearing headdresses from the wings of butterflies. Young people shouted and laughed, and sailed the lake in the shells of walnuts.

"We've chosen you, fair one," explained the very best-dressed fairy, "to deliver a message to the mortals. Right now the spring in which you seek dreams of your lover has no such power. It was us who caused your vision of Robin the Bowyer. But it would be a simple matter for us to charm the spring so that any maiden seeking knowledge of her future husband would have only to drop a sharp straight pin into the water, upon which she will see his face appear in the pool, or dream of him the next time she sleeps."

No sooner had the words been spoken when Joan grew drowsy and dropped into a heavy sleep, at which point the fairies carefully removed all the magic ointment from her eyes so that on awakening she would return to the world of mortals.

Ever since that magical day on the Hill of Brayton, young women have been dropping pins into spring wells across all of England, hoping for a glimpse of future lovers. 🌙

# WATER VISITS SUN

(NIGERIA)
*This story of Sun and Moon takes place before there were such beings as humans or birds or mammals, when the only life on earth was what lived in the sea. The story is popular with the Efik-Ibibo people, many of whom earn their livings— appropriately enough—as fishermen.*

N DAYS ALL BUT FORGOTTEN, Water and Sun not only both lived on earth; they were the best of friends. Many an afternoon did Sun take leave from his wife, Moon, to while away the hours talking and laughing with Water. But as the years went by, Sun grew increasingly disappointed with the fact that he was always the one doing the visiting, that never once had Water let him return the hospitality by coming to his house. "It would be a disaster!" Water cried when Sun offered the invitation. "It's not that I don't appreciate your kindness, but your house is far too small for all my people. If you want me to come, you must build the biggest courtyard you can imagine. Only then will you be safe."

"Say no more," said Sun, and off he went to build the biggest courtyard he could imagine. Every time he thought it was of sufficient size, Moon reminded him of what Water had said, and he took a deep breath, rolled up his sleeves, and made it even bigger. Finally, after weeks of construction, the compound was ready, and Sun hurried off to tell his friend.

"Are you certain it's all right for me to enter?" Water called to his friend from outside the gate, and Sun assured him it was. Slowly, in came Water and his people—the fish and the otter, the porpoise and the squid, the sea snake and the starfish and the barnacle. When Water had reached a depth of two or three feet, he called out again to his friend, "Are you certain it's still safe?" And Sun, wanting to be the very best of hosts, responded without the slightest hesitation. "Yes, yes, come in, all of you." So Water and his people carried on, and before long they were so deep that Sun and Moon had to stand on the roof of their house to be clear of them.

One final time Water asked if it was all right to continue, and one final time both Sun and his wife, Moon, bid him to hurry on. And with that Water overflowed the roof of the house, sending Sun and Moon fleeing into the sky, where they've been ever since. 𝄐

# THE BIRTH OF LIGHTNING

(LAOS)

*This wonderful little story anchors a great theme of many eastern religions: One evolves to true happiness—often over many lifetimes—by learning the value of generosity and by nurturing a willingness to celebrate life through selfless acts. Note how at the end the beautiful young maiden goes off with a wrinkled old man, choosing her partner not by his physical appeal, but by the quality of his heart. This is the point of early versions of "Cinderella"; the prince doesn't think twice about trying the glass slipper on a disheveled-looking hand-maiden (in fact, Cinderella), proving he's driven by a quest for inner, not outer, beauty.*

ONG AGO THERE LIVED a noble chief with ten wives, whose greatest pleasure in the world was to lay feasts for the poor. "You are an honorable man," the priests would tell him. "Surely you will be happy in the next life." While nine of the chief's wives saw the wisdom of such generosity—of "making merit," as it's often called—the tenth wife, the woman the chief adored most, wanted nothing to do with any of it.

In time those lives came to an end, as all life must, and on passing, the chief and the nine generous wives took their place in the heavens. But try as he might, the chief could not forget his favorite wife; most days would find him high in the clouds with looking glass in hand, scouting the far reaches of earth for some sign of her. One bright morning he was searching the shore of a remote lake, and lo and behold, there she was—she'd been reincarnated as a beautiful crane—walking along the edge of a marsh, looking for food. Then the chief did an amazing thing. Wanting to test the heart of his former wife, he changed himself into a fish and drifted over to where she was feeding. At first the crane pecked at the fish, but on realizing that it was alive, she turned away, even though she was terribly hungry. It was because she refused to take life, even though she was hungry, that the old chief knew her heart was good.

Not long after her life as a crane ended, the woman returned as the girl child of a humble gardener, and over the years grew to be as wise and fair as any woman in the land. When she reached marriage age, her parents threw a wonderful feast, during which they presented their daughter with a wreath of the finest flowers. "Toss this wreath into the air," her mother said, "and on whatever man's head it lands, that one shall be your husband."

Now unknown to anyone—for how could they suspect such a thing?—her former husband was at that feast, come to earth in the form of an old man. To everyone's horror, when the maiden closed her eyes and tossed the wreath high into the air, it was on his wrinkled, hairless head that it landed. "This can't be!" her father shouted. "The wreath must be thrown again!" His daughter, however, thought otherwise. She walked over to the old man, placed her hand in his, and together they rose into the sky. The girl's father was so outraged that he ran to the house, grabbed his gun, and tried to shoot the old man down!

Today when heat lightning flashes in the skies above Laos, the people may point and bid you to see that it is really the old man flashing his spotting scope across the earth, searching for his wife. Likewise, when spears of lightning strike at the forests, they may laugh and tell you it's nothing, just that foolish gardener, shooting at the old man who came to the feast and married his precious daughter. ☽

# SLEEP COMES FROM
# THE FLOWERS

(INDIA)

*People from the central regions of old India said flowers*
*weren't put on earth simply so humans could take delight in*
*them or even use them for adornment. Instead, blooming*
*plants were created so men and women would have something*
*of sufficient beauty to offer the gods.*

 ID YOU KNOW that when people first came
to live in the world they didn't know the simple
pleasure of sleep? They worked and then they
worked some more, even on dark nights when
there was no moon to light their toils. This greatly disturbed
the guiding spirit Nanga Baiga, who was wise enough to
know that everything in heaven and on earth needed rest.
But how to give slumber to humans?

Finally, one morning in early October, Nanga Baiga
decided to sprinkle a secret potion on the blooms of the
aconite flowers. Whenever the wind blew, it carried the
potion across the countryside and into the eyes of the people, causing them to fall into a deep, untroubled sleep. The
only problem was that the aconite flowers couldn't hold all
that much of the mixture; in a month it was gone, and the
people were right back to their restless ways. The solution,
Nanga Baiga decided, was to make sleep come from a different flower every month. And so it is today. In June the

people fall asleep at night from the spell cast by the unseen flower of the wild fig, while in July rest comes from the flowers of sarai. In the holy month of August slumber floats into the homes of the villagers from the blooms of the kir-sair, and in September from the delicate petals of sesamum. And on it goes through the year: sleep from saja flowers in November, and in December from the dhawar; in January from the tinsa, in February from the sargi, in March from the dehwan, April from the mango, May from the jamun. Thus it's thanks to Nanga Baiga—and of course to all these beautiful flowers—that the people find rest in all seasons. ☽

# THE COMING OF NIGHT

(BRAZIL)

*In some versions of this story, the curious servants who disobey orders and let night out of the bag are later changed into monkeys. Even today's monkeys bear a distinct mark on their lips—the same mark impressed in the sealing wax used to secure the flap on that bag full of night.*

**A**T THE BEGINNING of the world there was no such thing as night. The face of the sun was always full on the land, never rising and never setting, cloaking stars and moon alike. It was in these days that the lovely daughter of the Great Sea Serpent happened to fall in love with a human. In time they married, and the daughter bid farewell to her ocean home and went to live with her husband under the bright sun.

Though she was very much in love, living under the bright light of day was overwhelming to a being used to the shadows of the sea. As the months passed she grew withdrawn, despondent. "There's something in my father's kingdom we call night," she told her worried husband. "It's a soothing darkness, a fabric woven out of heavy shadows under which you can rest your eyes, where you can sleep without burden. If only I could have a little night."

On hearing this, the husband rose from his wife's bedside, ran from their home, and summoned three of his most trustworthy servants. "I have urgent business for you," he told them. "You must travel to the kingdom of the Great Sea Serpent and tell him that his daughter is in dire need of darkness. Tell him she may die here if she can't gain a slice of night." And off they ran to the sea.

On hearing this troubling news, the Great Sea Serpent hurried off into the shadows to fill a bag with night, sealed it tight, then gave it to the servants. "Remember one thing," he told the three men. "Whatever you do, don't open this bag until you reach my daughter."

This sounds like a simple enough task. True, the bag was heavy, but these were strong men, used to carrying such weight on their heads for miles at a time. But what unraveled them were the strange sounds coming from that bag full of night: the piercing cries of night birds and the drone of insects, a chorus of hoots and howls unlike anything they'd ever heard. Two of the men were tempted to simply drop the bag and run for home. But one of the servants was more curious than alarmed, and after much persuading, convinced his partners that they should open the bag to see what was causing all the commotion. So they laid it on the ground and broke the Serpent's wax seal. In a wink all the birds and bugs and beasts spilled out, wrapped in a huge cloud of night.

Back in the village, Sea Serpent's daughter sat under a royal palm tree, waiting for the servants' return. Shortly after the bag was opened, she happened to raise her tired eyes and see the mist of night gathering on the horizon. With a happy sigh she lay down under the palm and fell into a blissful sleep.

She awoke in that time between darkness and dawn,

healthy, filled with joy. A princess again. As she walked, she spoke to those things that would become key players in the hours between dusk and morning. She told the rooster it would be his job to keep watch and call out at the approach of day. Likewise, she spoke to the star we know as morning star, giving it her blessing to rule the sky just before dawn. So many birds she commanded to sing their finest songs in those magic hours.

It's thanks to night spilling out at the hands of those servants that in Brazil darkness rolls quickly over the earth; it's because of them that the creatures of the night break into a loud chorus at the first sign of the setting sun. ☽

# THE LOST VOICE OF PISO LAKE

(LIBERIA)

*Local storytellers say that Piso Lake was at one time but a jumble of water holes, made by tens of thousands of doves that flocked there to bathe and sing. Then came the time of the big rains, and the water holes were joined into a single lake dotted with beautiful islands. On remarkable days one of these islands—Booka, named after the owner of the world—drifts about the lake, searching for something humans cannot fathom.*

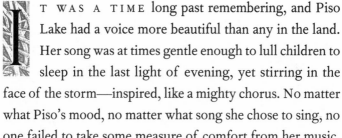 T WAS A TIME long past remembering, and Piso Lake had a voice more beautiful than any in the land. Her song was at times gentle enough to lull children to sleep in the last light of evening, yet stirring in the face of the storm—inspired, like a mighty chorus. No matter what Piso's mood, no matter what song she chose to sing, no one failed to take some measure of comfort from her music. One day the Sea, who lived nearby, came to visit Piso, and his heart was heavy. "The Goddess of the Sea is dying," he told the lake. "As you must know, I have no proper voice of my own with which to mourn her. I beg you—might I borrow yours?" Of course, what could Piso do but give her voice to the Sea? What no one could have imagined, though, was that the song Sea carried to his love—Piso's song—was so beautiful, so compelling, that instead of dying, the goddess rose from that dark place and came back to life.

But ah, that cunning Sea! When Piso asked for her voice back, he refused, saying he'd borrowed it as a song for mourning the death of the goddess, and therefore it couldn't be returned until the goddess actually died. And who could say when that would be? Today sailors talk much about the haunting songs of the ocean. How thrilling they are. How enchanting. But what they're really hearing is the voice of Piso, the voice that once stirred the people of Liberia, lulled their children to sleep in the last light of evening. ☽

# WIND TEACHES
# HEALING

(POMO INDIANS, NORTH-CENTRAL CALIFORNIA)
*Few cultures have been better at preserving their myths than the Pomo Indians—something accomplished for many centuries by oral tradition alone. There's an uncanny familiarity among many Pomo tales—an ancient flood, people living in a paradise-like garden, and as the ancient Celts believed, the spirit crossing a narrow bridge over a deep chasm to reach the hereafter.*

FOR THIS TALE we must return to a spring long passed, when fire still burned in the crown of the sacred mountain Konocti, when flowers first found the cool shores of the Big Water, Ka-Batin. In those days lived a chief whose life was pulled by the songs of the wind—who filled the hours of his days at the edge of the canyons or on the tops of mountains—listening, trying to catch the words, hoping to see the face of the singer. But in all that time the only word he ever understood was *Wintun*, and it was by this name he became known. Over the years, Wintun's father grew more and more concerned about his son's refusal to spend time at the *lamah*, or roundhouse, where he would learn the healing songs of his people.

In time Wintun passed away, leaving only his son, Young Wintun. Just like his father had done, Young Wintun spent little time in the roundhouse practicing religion, preferring instead to sit in the flowered meadows at the foot of Konocti and listen to the wind. Decades passed and one by one the people of his tribe died, until only Wintun was left, an old man himself. Sick and frail, in the season when snow hides the earth, Wintun crawled out of the lodge, hoping to come across something he could eat. Out on the wind-driven snow he found a robin with a broken wing. "I'm so hungry," he told the bird. "But I can hardly eat you, for you're in even worse shape than me." He tucked the bird against his breast and crawled back to the dying fire in his lodge to mend the robin's broken wing. In just a few days, not only the bird but Wintun, too, had gained a new measure of strength, and he was again able to care for himself.

Still more years passed, and now Wintun was a very old man, again barely hanging on, weak and suffering and crawling through the snow hoping to find morsels of food. One day he was out searching when suddenly he heard the wind's voice calling his name. Turning, he saw that there stood the robin whose wing he'd mended years ago. So this was the face of the wind spirit! "You helped me when I was injured," said the bird, "warmed me and bound my wing. And now I will help you." And with that the robin hopped over and began to sing his healing song, and Wintun felt the strength of it.

And when he'd moved back from death's door, Wintun set off to find the remaining tribes of the Pomo, sat with them and taught them the robin's healing song. It's that song that has been sung in roundhouses ever since, always in the spring, after the wind has come and pushed away the dark and cold. 🐦

# THE HIDDEN PEOPLE

(ICELAND)

*Cultures around the world have long claimed the presence of
elves, or other elusive creatures akin to humans. It's interesting to note that throughout much of Europe this same story
was often used to explain the differences between ethnic or
social classes.*

OU'LL SEE THEM only if they want you
to, and even then, more often than not it will be
just for a split second, out of the corner of
your eye, among the woods and moors, in the
rocks and cliffs and caves along the cold shores of Iceland.
The elves. Or, more politely, the hidden people.

A long time ago the Lord God Himself came down to
earth to visit Adam and Eve. As you might imagine, these
two were beside themselves, joyful for the visit, but terribly
nervous. Adam suggested they begin with a tour of the yard
and the gardens, the house and woods and the fish in the
clear-running streams, all of which God was eager to see.
And then the children. Eve brought them out from the
kitchen, scrubbed clean, smiles on their faces. Each was
beautiful, a pleasure for all to see, including God. "Have you
any other children?" God finally asked. "No," said Eve.
"No, this is all of them."

But it wasn't true. There were in fact other children—several more—but because Eve hadn't gotten around to bathing

them, she was ashamed and didn't want God to see. God knew she'd hidden them, though, and before he left, he turned to Adam and Eve and said something they did not understand at the time: "What you've hidden from me will also be hidden from men."

And thus it was that human beings descended from the children shown to God, while the elves, or hidden people of nature, came from those children who were kept from His sight. Ever since, humans have had a feeling of uncertainty, even fear about the hidden people. Some say it's because of the strange powers they possess, but maybe there's also some lingering shame, some haunting regret for having hidden those dear children from the face of God. 𝔇

# THE PIPES OF PAN

(ANCIENT GREECE)

*Writer Henry Miller once said that while the Greek gods may have died, we still feel their presence. Indeed, their tracks are everywhere, especially in our language—in our words for the months of the year and the days of the week, as well as in countless terms used in psychology, biology, and medicine.*

ANY ARE THE TALES of the Greek god Pan, half man and half goat. Pan was an exuberant god, reveling in erotic pleasures by night, by day taking long naps on the sunlit slopes of the ancient world. So thoroughly did Pan treasure these afternoon siestas that at midday hunters and animals alike would lie low, too, lest they accidentally rouse him, provoking one of his sour moods. It was the fear of this foul temper, first suffered in the woods and fields of Greece, that gave us our word *PANic*.

Pan's sexual appetite would at times drive him like a moth to flame. Over the years he lay with thousands of nymphs, including Echo, whom Hera had cursed for helping hide her husband's philandering; deprived of all speech, Echo could only repeat the last word of whoever was talking to her. Also favored by Pan were the Maenads, or "the frenzied ones," so named because they followed the drunken Dionysus, roaming the countryside as he taught humans the art of making wine.

Yet all this isn't to suggest that Pan wasn't capable of deep affection. He had great love, for instance, for the lovely nymph Syrinx. Spying her one day on the top of Mount Lyceum, Pan took chase, at which point Syrinx sped down the mountain and into the River Laedon. Just as Pan was about to pluck her from the waters, she veered for the riverbank and turned herself into a reed. Try as he might, poor Pan just couldn't distinguish Syrinx from the rest of the reeds growing along the shoreline. As a way of consoling himself, he selected several reeds at random and used them to fashion a flute, or "Pan-pipe." The music that poured from that instrument was pure magic—so marvelous, in fact, that King Midas once judged it more beautiful than Apollo's lyre.

Given the enchanting qualities of Pan's flute, it seems only appropriate that centuries later, when zoologists were scratching their heads over what name to give to the windpipe of songbirds, they settled on *syrinx*. ♪)

# THE HEALING WATERS

(IROQUOIS, NORTHEASTERN UNITED STATES)
*Virtually all the world's mythologies assign some measure*
*of healing power to springs. Indeed, if Mother Earth symbol-*
*izes the forces of creation, then the nurturing of the life she*
*engenders can be said to come through the gifts of the spring.*
*As a psychological notion, dream images of springs are often*
*treated as healing symbols of the unconscious. Like the Iro-*
*quois in the story that follows, all people sometimes suffer*
*from plagues of the heart; in the end we must make a heroic*
*inner journey to find the source of wellness.*

 ONG AGO A fierce winter fell upon the North-east; in its arms was a terrible plague that threatened to destroy the Iroquois Nation. Young Nekumonta watched in horror as first his parents died, then his sisters and brothers and his two young children. And then his beautiful wife, Shanewis, whom he loved more than life itself, caught the sickness, too, and she began to prepare herself for her journey to the land of the dead. His heart nearly broken, Nekumonta gathered his courage one bitter morning and walked off into the dark heart of the forest, determined to find where the Great Manitou had planted His healing herbs.

For three days and nights Nekumonta wandered the woods through deep snow, often on his hands and knees, trying to catch either sight or scent of the healing plants. Often he would ask for help from the animals of the forest—the rabbit and the bear, the deer and the moose—but all just looked away, saddened by the hopelessness of his task. By the third night, Nekumonta was so tired and hungry that at one point he tripped over a branch and simply laid where he fell, too exhausted to get up. The creatures of the woods gathered at his side and watched over him as he slept. Each one of them had known Nekumonta to be a sympathetic man—a compassionate hunter, a protector of the flowers and the trees. In their pity for him the animals began to cry to the Great Manitou in one voice, praying that Shanewis would be healed. And Manitou heard.

As Nekumonta lay sleeping, Manitou dispatched a messenger to bring a dream. It began with a clear vision of his wife singing a beautiful song that sounded like running water. In time the image of Shanewis melted away, replaced by a spring. The spring called softly to Nekumonta, telling him that in its waters he would find the promise of new life.

He awoke and looked all around him, but Nekumonta could see no water. When he cocked his head, though, he began to hear faint whispers from a spring, sounds that seemed to be coming from a place directly beneath his feet. And so with tree branch and flint, Nekumonta dug and scraped through the frozen earth, hour after hour, until finally he reached the loveliest of springs, its banks crowded with life. First he bathed his aching body, and in a matter of minutes felt strong again. After giving thanks, he fashioned a jar of clay, hardened it in a roaring fire, then filled it with the life-giving water.

Upon returning to his village, Nekumonta gave the weary

people directions to the spring and then hurried off to his wife. Some of the water he poured between her lips, and the rest he used to gently bathe her hands and brow until she fell into a peaceful slumber. When she awoke, the fever was gone.

And so the people gave Nekumonta the title Chief of the Healing Waters so that all who came after would know who had carried this precious gift to the Iroquois. ☽

# THE FOREST
# AND THE TIGER

(JAVA, INDONESIA)

*There is no simpler and yet more poignant story about the consequences of letting anger or alienation push us into solitary paths, abandoning the riches that come with friendship and community.*

IN THE BEGINNING Forest and Tiger were the best of friends. They would talk of this and that, but mainly they just liked being together, watching the coming and going of the seasons, tracking the roll of sun and moon as they slipped across the sky, high above the branches of the trees. With the coming of humans, the two friends came to appreciate each other even more. You see, people were reluctant to come and cut down the trees because they feared being eaten by the Tiger; likewise, when humans came with spears determined to hunt down tiger, it was the shadows of the forest that allowed him to stay free from harm.

But as sometimes happens even with good friends, the day came when these two began taking each other for granted. That, in time, led to feelings of resentment, even contempt. "You do little here with your presence but foul my beautiful floor," Forest said to Tiger one day. Tiger, in turn, scoffed at the forest for its dark and gloomy thickets, saying how troublesome such a place was, how difficult it was to warm his back in the fingers of sun. One day Tiger simply walked away, out into the world of open hills and valleys.

It wasn't long, of course, before humans discovered that the forest was no longer guarded. They rushed in and cut down trees like there was no tomorrow, until the once-beautiful forest was nothing but a barren, lifeless place. Sadly, the tiger fared no better. Because he was unable to hide in those shadowy thickets, the men with spears found him easily, killing him and his kind by the hundreds. And thus what had at first seemed like nothing more than an unfortunate parting of ways between friends was in fact the beginning of the end, the undoing of both the forest and the tiger. 🌙